So You're Sayin' I'm Bitter?

(Doing Forgiveness— God's Way)

By Dr. Don Dunlap
Lulu Publishing, Inc.
Morrisville, NC

☐

SO YOU'RE SAYIN' I'M BITTER?
(DOING FORGIVENESS—GOD'S WAY)
Published by Lulu Publishers, Inc.
3131 RDU Center, Suite 210
Morrisville, NC 27560

Printed in the United States of America

ISBN 1-4116-2924-8

All Scripture references are used by permission from the New American Standard Bible, copyright © The Lockman Foundation, 1960, 1962, 1963, 1968, 1971, 1972, 1973, 1975, 1977. Used by permission. The King James Version. The Message, copyright © 1993. Used by permission.

Details in some anecdotes and stories have been changed to protect the identities of the persons involved.

A Word About Using Case Studies

The use of case studies is a helpful tool for effectively communicating the truths of biblical forgiveness. In an effort to protect the identity and privacy of the people involved, I've intentionally changed many of the facts. Some of the studies are composites of several counseling situations.

For example, if I tell you about a grandfather who sexually molested his granddaughter, I assure you that, tragically, there have been many such situations that I've dealt with throughout the years of my counseling ministry. Although I've changed some of the details and combined some of the circumstances, I believe I've related the true essence of each of the case studies we will review.

Preface

During the past 25 years, I've conducted approximately 25,000 counseling appointments, the majority of which addressed general marriage and family problems. The rest covered a wide range of issues such as overcoming depression and anxiety, discerning God's will, and learning financial stewardship.

Throughout the course of these sessions, one problem has surfaced more often than any: Most Christians have a serious misunderstanding of the process of biblical forgiveness. Forgiveness involves our relationship with God, as well as with others. Before we begin the counseling process, I often ask counselees to define biblical forgiveness. Most seem confident that they know the definition, yet I hardly ever receive the right answer.

Knowing how to forgive is what I call a prerequisite skill for living a successful life. The truths of biblical forgiveness form the foundation for most of what gets accomplished in my counseling practice. Whatever problem a person is dealing with, whether marriage problems, a stressful job or a rebellious teenager, he will discover how to face the conflict and handle the hurts and frustrations when he learns to fogive God's way.

If fact, I'm convinced that until a follower of Christ learns and applies the principles of biblical forgiveness, his life is destined for shipwreck.

Acknowledgements

I want to thank the many counselees who've been faithful to apply God's solutions to their problems. It's a great blessing to be an eye-witness to God's transforming power in each of your lives.

Thanks to the staff of Christianity.com who provided the encouragement and opportunity to write this book while I worked for you—Dale, Sandy, Rick, and especially Dr. Terry Dorian. More than anyone, you believed this project could be accomplished and urged me to move forward with the effort.

Thanks to my parents who've always believed the best in me and who've supported me in every goal I've ever reached for.

Deepest thanks to my wife and children who are living testimonies of what it means to live, love, laugh, play, pray, sing, worship, and most of all, forgive. (I hope you've forgiven me for making you sit through countless sermons on forgiveness.)

Table of Contents

Chapter 1

Introduction to Forgiveness

Most Christians today are confused when it comes to understanding what biblical forgiveness actually is.

Why is it important to have a clear understanding of biblical forgiveness? First, refusing to forgive is a sin. Second, unforgiveness results in some of the most severe emotional and spiritual problems a person can experience. When we don't understand how to forgive others biblically, we forfeit the benefits we could otherwise derive from our trials.

Forgiveness is one of the most misunderstood topics of our day. Ask a group of ten Christians how the Bible defines forgiveness, and you'll likely get ten different answers. Some may answer that forgiveness is choosing not to hold someone accountable for his offense. Others would suggest we seek forgiveness for offenses by apologizing to the person we offended. Still others, who've bought into the popular no-fault philosophy, might reply that people who love each other should never have to say they're sorry for anything.

Knowing how to forgive is a life-skill.

When someone learns to forgive the way God forgives, he becomes equipped with the necessary skills to deal with conflict as it arises on any front—in his home, his church, and his community.

Who would deny that our society is slowly strangling in the grasp of the rampant anger and hostility that threaten to unravel us at our cultural seams? The alarming incidence of child abuse and domestic violence, as well as the tragic reality of countless students murdering each other in our public schools, all point to the fact that the majority of people don't understand how to apply the principles of authentic forgiveness to their daily lives.

Is anyone out there guilty?

Our no-fault society is another factor that clouds the issue of true forgiveness. It seems no one today is responsible for his choices. A victim mentality has infected our nation. We blame someone's wrong actions, for example, on his poor upbringing: "He robbed a bank because his parents didn't give him an allowance when he was a kid." Or we look for some excuse to explain away destructive behavior: "She got drunk and wrecked her car because her boyfriend dumped her." "He went on a killing rampage because his boss pushed him over the edge." It has become socially unacceptable to label any evildoer guilty.

We must take responsibility for our choices.

The words of Galatians 6:7,8 clearly reveal God's opinion of our skewed understanding of personal responsibility for sin: "Do not be deceived, God is not mocked; for whatever a man sows, this he will also reap. For the one who sows to his own flesh, shall from the flesh reap corruption, but the one who sows to the Spirit, shall from the Spirit, reap eternal life." Where sin is concerned, God does *not* condone blame-placing. We *are* responsible for the choices we make in life—choices that bear lasting consequences.

God expects His children to take responsibility for every thought, every word, and every action. When we have a clear understanding of biblical forgiveness, we move from the deception of a victim mentality to the acceptance of personal responsibility for every aspect of our lives.

God is strong in our weakness.

At several junctures in my Christian life, I've nearly succumbed to the belief that my unwise choices and sinful behavior had rendered me worthless to God, and useless to the Body of Christ. Yet, repeatedly, God in His mercy has faithfully proven Himself strong in my weakness.

The powerful words of encouragement found in 2 Corinthians 1:3,4, constitute the basis for my counseling ministry: "Blessed be the God and Father of our Lord Jesus Christ, the Father of mercies and God of all comfort; who comforts us in all our affliction so that we may be able to comfort those who are in any affliction, with the comfort with which we ourselves are comforted by God."

I have often personally experienced the comfort described in these verses, as the Lord has graciously granted me His forgiveness for my transgressions against Him. One of the compelling goals of my life and ministry is to share that glorious comfort with hurting people.

As Christ's appointed ambassadors in this world, we are called to be effective people-helpers. Once we master the truths of biblical forgiveness, we can use this vital information as a resource with which to help countless other people. And the ultimate result? God will receive honor and glory!

We need to learn to deal with any difficult situation in life in a way that wins God's commendations.

To be conscious of God means that we maintain the awareness that God is present in the midst of every problem. When we're conscious of God, we view each trial with God's perspective, and we acknowledge that in each difficulty we face, God is up to a specific work in our lives. As we respond biblically to our trials, the people God has placed in our life will note our God-given ability to persevere. And if we persevere in faith, God stands ready to commend us for responding obediently to His commands.

We begin our consideration of biblical forgiveness with a passage from 1 Peter 2:19:"It is commendable, if because he is conscious of God, a man bears up under sorrows when suffering unjustly." Whatever trying circumstances we're walking through, whatever hurts we're experiencing, whether in our personal relationships, our jobs or our health, we're to be commended if we're bearing up under them. This passage reveals the only way we're able to bear up under our trials: "because you are conscious of God."

Is God applauding you?

The literal meaning of the word commend is "to clap." When a Greek or Roman athlete won a sporting competition, the crowds would cheer and applaud his victory. When God allows us to go through the difficult situations we face, He stands ready to commend us if we don't grow fainthearted in the race.

Do you have a sense today that God is commending you for the way you're dealing with the problems in your marriage? What about the problems associated with your workplace? Are you experiencing God's commendations for your Christ-like attitude toward that rebellious teenager? If not, be assured that you can learn to deal with any difficult situation of life in such a way that will win God's commendations.

Several years ago my counseling office was located in a medical building in Greenville, South Carolina. I recall the first time I drove onto the facility grounds. I was awestruck by the beauty! With its colorful flowers and manicured lawn, the landscaping surrounding the building reminded me of Disney World. Behind the building, however, was an ugly drainage ditch, visible only from an inside office window.

Often, after I had read 1 Peter 2:19 to a counselee, I would lead him to that window and ask him to look out and describe what he saw. As the counselee viewed the slimy green water with beer cans and filth floating around in it, the response was generally something like, "Yuk!"

Then I would tell him the ditch represents the life of someone who has very little joy or peace. I would then say that our goal in the counseling process was to take him on a pilgrimage. By the end of our sessions together, we would figuratively work our way around to the other side of the building where everything looked beautiful, smelled good, and was in every way, appealing.

We must embark on a journey to a new perspective.

God desires to rescue each of His children from the cesspool of sinful behavior and an unforgiving heart. He promises to take us to a place where we will have peace beyond comprehension. He wants to give us a wellspring of joy that bubbles up within us. Best of all, when we learn to forgive as He forgives, God will grant us a deep, abiding contentment regardless of our earthly circumstances.

Forgiveness is a word that must be carefully defined according to God's Word, because many dangerous deceptions masquerade as biblical forgiveness. The primary objective of the Enemy of Our Faith is to convince us that certain things are true when they are not. We must expose these deceptions and establish biblical truths in order to set people free from the hurts and offenses they encounter in life.

Teachers often give their students a pretest before they introduce a new concept. The scores, not surprisingly, are generally low. Then after the teacher teaches the concept, he administers the test again to get an indication of how much the students learned from the presentation. If the students are attentive and the teacher has done his job well, the re-test usually results in significantly higher scores.

In the same way, you may not fully understand the definition of forgiveness at the beginning of our investigation. However, I urge you to keep this definition before you, and it should become increasingly clearer to you as we progress in our study.

The Definition of Biblical Forgiveness

Biblical forgiveness involves our correct responses to God when people offend us. Offenses are the wrongs that others inflict upon us—the hurts, the frustrations, the irritations. Offenses are those things that cause us hardship and grief. This definition will be restated several times throughout the course of our study, and we'll attempt to apply the definition to specific situations which may be occurring in your life.

Most Christians have a shallow understanding of forgiveness.

It's important to begin by pointing out some wrong definitions of biblical forgiveness. If the Father of Lies can succeed in blinding a Christian to the truth of biblical forgiveness, he can render him incapable of truly forgiving offenders.

A superficial understanding of forgiveness abounds in the evangelical church today. Many Christians settle for a shallow grasp of this issue. They never go on to master the truths necessary to derive the full benefit from their problems. Therefore, we must expose these deceptions and establish biblical truths in order their place.

Many people in Christian vocations don't understand forgiveness.

There's another reason why Christians should be made aware of the forgiveness deceptions posing as truth. Approximately one-third of my counseling clientele over the last decade have been pastors, church staff members, missionaries, and para-church personnel. Almost without exception, when I mention their need to forgive someone they announce rather indignantly, "Well, I already understand all about forgiveness." Perhaps they've preached a sermon on forgiveness or maybe they've helped someone else work through the need to forgive an offender. They believe they are experts on this subject.

With this in mind, I designed the first section of this book to help people who work in vocational Christian ministry come to the realization that there may be some aspects of the forgiveness process they haven't considered, or don't yet fully understand. I've found that after I question these individuals for two or three minutes, it becomes evident that most of them have failed to apply many important aspects of the forgiveness process.

When I begin to expose the various deceptions that obstruct the path of true biblical forgiveness, however, I don't often get much resistance from pastors and other Christian workers regarding their need to take a fresh look at the forgiveness issue.

Chapter 2

God's Bigger Than My Offender

Forgiveness Deception #1: Offenders act solely on their own initiative.

Our beliefs about God's role in our lives can close us off or open us up to the many benefits of biblical forgiveness. Those who believe this first deception, assume that an offender perpetrates his offense exclusively on his own authority and by his own motivation. In short, his choice to commit an offense is the only reason the offense occurred. This belief is a natural assumption of the human heart. Thus, when someone hurts us, we focus on the bad treatment we've suffered. Soon the hurt turns to anger and seething resentment. Before long, bitterness takes root in our hearts.

Do we believe God's in charge?

To get at the truth regarding biblical forgiveness a Christian must first ask himself, "Do I belong to God? Am I confident that Jesus Christ is in my life? Am I willing to submit my life to His authority?" If Jesus Christ is not your Lord and if you're not willing to submit your life to His leadership, the promises contained in the scriptural principles of forgiveness don't apply to you.

However, if you answered "yes" to the above questions, God desires to establish a very important truth in your heart. It's interesting to note that Baptists, Methodists, Presbyterians, and Roman Catholics are all in agreement on this particular truth, which is found in the Bible from Genesis 1 all the way through Revelation 22. The truth is that God is in charge.

To use scriptural terminology, we say that God is *sovereign*. Because God is sovereign, nothing can touch our life unless God first authorizes it. A sovereign God, who can prevent an offense from touching us, must therefore allow the offense to reach us before it can hurt us. When God chooses not to stop an offense, it is because He desires to use it to benefit our lives. He knows that the pain we endure will result in our ultimate good. The implications here are obvious. Our problems are bigger than whatever our husband or wife has done to offend us. They are bigger than our employer's angry attitudes. They are bigger than the unfair treatment we're getting from our parents.

God is interested in how we respond to our offenders.

Although God is intimately acquainted with every detail of His children's afflictions and hardships, He is far more concerned with how we respond to our problems, trials, and difficulties. (He is very concerned, as well, about the offenders, the perpetrators and the victimizers. He has a plan for them too.) The way in which we respond to offenses, however, is probably the greatest determining factor of whether Jesus Christ is Lord of our lives or whether we are retaining some aspects of that control for ourselves.

No circumstance we've ever been through has touched our lives by chance. No situation we've ever faced has occurred by accident. No difficulty we've ever encountered has happened apart from divine will. In Romans 8:28 we find a powerful promise to every Believer, "We know that God causes all things to work together for good to those who love God, to those who are called according to His purpose." God has promised to bring good out of every offense that we have ever endured.

God is on His throne and He will bring specific good out of every trial we go through.

God is present in every difficult situation we face. In Isaiah 45:7,9,11, we learn that the same God who forms the light and who brings prosperity also *creates disaster*. We must trust that God is in loving control of our lives, that He has a plan for us, and that He will bring specific good out of every trial.

As we consider God's sovereign goodness in every circumstance of a Christian's life, it would stand to reason that someone might ask, for example, "What possible good could come from the sexual molestation of a child?" "What could ever be considered good about a father tragically drowning in a boating accident?" "Could any good come out of a situation where a wife has suffered at the hands of a raging, drunken husband, or worse yet, a husband who is *not* drunk?" Yet, God is able to bring about good in each one of these situations, in a way that may not be clear at first. Our goal as we continue our discussion of biblical forgiveness is to further clarify this truth.

God is on His throne and no detail escapes His attention.

God is present in every difficult situation that His children must face. He is up to great things in the midst of each circumstance. The writer of Isaiah 45:7,9,11 reiterates this pivotal truth: "I form the light and create darkness. I bring prosperity and create disaster; I, the Lord, do all these things. Woe to him who quarrels with his Maker, to him who is but a potsherd among the potsherds on the ground. Does the clay say to the potter, 'What are you making?' This is what the Lord says—the Holy One of Israel, and its Maker: Concerning things to come, do you question Me about My children, or give Me orders about the work of My hands?"

We must pay careful attention to these verses. God is doing the talking here. Few Christians would argue with the first part of this passage which affirms God as the one who causes the sun to rise each morning and to set each evening. God goes on to tell us, "I bring prosperity." This scripture confirms the fact that every good and perfect gift we receive comes from above. The next part of the first verse is what many Christians refuse to believe: "I [God] create disaster." The same God who forms the light, who creates the darkness and who brings prosperity, also creates disaster.

The Lord is a Shepherd who knows how to guide our lives.

Verses 9 and 10 are wonderfully versatile. I often say to a disgruntled wife, "Woe to him who quarrels with his Maker…Does the clay say to the potter, 'Why did you give me this husband?' 'Why did you give me these teenagers?' " God will not be challenged as to His plans for His children. He won't be given orders concerning the work of His hands. He reminds us in these verses that every good thing we already have is in some way related to His grace. He tells us to trust Him because He knows what He is doing in the midst of this disaster.

God is lovingly in control of every detail of our lives.

He is there. Sometimes we cannot feel Him there, but He is there. His promise to us is that He is in charge. He offers us this glorious reassurance in Zephaniah 3:17, "The Lord your God is with you, He is mighty to save. He will take great delight in you, He will quiet you with His love, He will rejoice over you with singing." God is on His throne, and He will bring specific good out of every trial that we are going through.

Chapter 3

What If I Don't Feel Hurt?

Forgiveness Deception #2: I've forgiven someone who offended me because I no longer have hurt feelings toward him.

Many Christians believe they've forgiven an offender because they are no longer experiencing hurt feelings. But the truth is, if we fail to truly forgive, we will continue to suffer emotional, spiritual, and physical consequences long after the actual feelings of hurt have subsided.

We shouldn't assume we've forgiven someone simply because we no longer harbor *feelings* of hurt. Someone who is currently going through a difficult situation may be experiencing deep feelings of hurt and bitterness. However, if the offense took place in a person's life years ago, such as events that happened when he was a child, the painful emotions that he once experienced may have long since subsided.

I recently spoke at a workshop attended by about 100 people. At one point in the presentation I asked, "How many of you remember specific offenses your parents committed against you while you were growing up?" To get them thinking, I suggested perhaps there had been conflict in their home, or maybe their parents had been guilty of anger or harsh discipline.

I went on to explain that the problem may not have been so much the things their parents had *done* to hurt them—maybe they had good parents who took them to church and who were faithful to one another—but that possibly, the offenses grew out of the things their parents had *not* done, that they *should* have done.

Parents are called to raise their children in the nurture and admonition of the Lord.

We know from Scripture that in order to raise a child in the nurture and admonition of the Lord, a Christian parent must fulfill certain obligations. So I asked the workshop attendees some further questions: "Did your parents teach you how to pray? Do you remember listening to your parents' prayers? Did your family have consistent family worship? Did you read God's Word and seek His guidance together as a family? Were you taught to memorize Scripture and get it deep in your heart and soul, so it was there to draw upon in times of temptation and difficulty during those critical teenage years? To summarize, did your parents *not* do some things they should have done?"

After I explained my questions to the workshop participants, I asked everyone in attendance to close their eyes. Then I said, "Based on these questions I've asked you, (things done and things left undone) how many of you were offended by your parents while you were growing up?" Almost everyone in the auditorium raised their hands.

It is possible to be unforgiving toward someone and not be aware of it.

Then I asked this follow-up question: "Now that you are adults, many of you married with children of your own, how many of you still have hurt *feelings* toward your parents today?" I was not at all surprised by the response. Only one man raised his hand. In the same way that feelings of grief gradually diminish in their intensity, feelings of hurt tend to dissipate with the passing of time. This is especially true if the offenses are no longer ongoing.

So the mistaken conclusion that is often reached, particularly by Christians, is this: "Because the offenses took place a long time ago and because I no longer feel hurt or resentful toward my offender, I know that I've forgiven him." It is crucially important, however, to understand the truth of the matter. Even though someone believes he has forgiven an offender, he will experience long-lasting adverse effects in life if he doesn't learn how to forgive biblically.

When we fail to thoroughly apply the principles of biblical forgiveness to each offense we encounter, we'll continue to suffer emotional, spiritual, and physical consequences long after the actual feelings of hurt have subsided.

This case study involves a woman who came to me with a marriage problem. She was very unhappy in her relationship with her husband. They were both committed Christians who had been married for several years, and they had three children. Her husband was very gifted and active in church ministry. She told me she was on the verge of asking her husband to leave. She said, "This is so unlike me. I can't believe I'm even thinking about this, much less expressing it to a counselor."

When I asked her what the problem was she said, "He's often harsh and angry and he loses his temper at the slightest provocation. He yells at me; he yells at the kids, and it's affecting my love for him." She went on to explain that the affection she once felt for him was almost gone. She told me, "I don't want him to touch me, especially after he's been harsh." Her husband, like most men, wanted to hug and kiss her as a way to "make up" after they had an argument.

His wife and children dreaded his frequent bouts of anger.

She continued, "I'm seeing the effect his anger is having on the children. They're afraid of him. One of the worst things about his outbursts is that we all have to walk on eggshells to prevent setting him off. Another thing I've noticed is that when he's not around, the children have begun to express that same kind of anger toward one another." She concluded with the statement, "I just don't think I can take it anymore. I know Christians are not supposed to separate, but I'm ready to ask him to leave."

Too many husbands wait until the situation is desperate to call for help.

Many husbands agree to go for counseling only after their wives have threatened to leave them. It is a sad and unfortunate truth that when a man's back is against the wall, he becomes willing to consider what he must to save his marriage. That's what happened in this situation when she asked her husband to leave. He saw his wife's desperation and the seriousness of his sin. Finally realizing for the first time that his anger could lead to the loss of his wife and children, this man agreed to go for counseling. He came to see me and we began the task of exposing the deceptions this husband had believed for years regarding true biblical forgiveness.

The wife believed her husband had not forgiven his father for his anger.

As we began the first counseling session, the wife made an interesting comment that gave me insight into her husband's problem. She told me she believed the sin of anger was deeply rooted in her husband's family. His father was a very angry man who had treated his mother harshly and who had consistently demonstrated angry attitudes toward him and his siblings. For example, when his father couldn't get a confession from his children for some wrong that had been committed, he would line them up and spank them all to make sure he had "gotten" the guilty party.

The husband didn't agree with his wife's theory.

When I suggested that we needed to take a closer look at how his father's anger had influenced his life, her husband strongly objected to my idea. "I haven't had a conflict with my father since I moved away from home 25 years ago," he protested. "I love my father. I have a better relationship with him now than I ever had growing up, and I'm certain that I don't have any resentment or animosity toward him." He continued, "I honestly don't believe my problem with anger has anything to do with my father. I will listen to what you have to say, but I don't think it applies to my situation."

He hadn't really forgotten the offenses from his childhood days.

Part of the process of biblical forgiveness involves enumerating exactly what the offenses are so a person can consciously and deliberately forgive each offense. When we came to this point in the counseling process, I asked him to list the specific offenses his father had committed against him while he was growing up. He answered, "I don't think I can remember any."

Yet two and a half hours later we had written several pages of offenses. He hadn't really forgotten the vacations they had taken as a family when his dad would get angry in the middle of the trip and take them home several days early. He hadn't forgotten the tears in his mother's eyes when his father would shout angrily at her. He hadn't forgotten what it felt like to be unjustly disciplined for things he hadn't done.

He finally overcame life-dominating sins of harshness and anger.

Although this husband had been a successful Christian leader for many years, he went through the biblical process of forgiving his father for the first time in his life. In the weeks and months that followed, he experienced a desire and power from the Lord, as never before, to overcome the life-dominating sins of harshness and anger.

This man, who had vehemently disagreed with my initial suggestion concerning the root cause of his anger, came to clearly understand that he had believed a deception regarding forgiveness. Despite his belief that he harbored no feelings of hurt or bitterness towards his father, he had never, prior to the time we met together, biblically forgiven him.

He realized for the first time that his lack of forgiveness had produced negative effects in the lives of his wife and children long after his feelings of hurt toward his father had subsided. Once he understood how his anger was crippling his family, he was eager to expose the deception he had believed, and he was ready to implement the principles of genuine forgiveness.

Chapter 4

The Accountability Issue

Forgiveness Deception #3: I've forgiven someone because I choose not to hold him accountable any longer for his offense.

The commonly held belief that biblical forgiveness occurs when an offended person chooses not to hold the offender accountable any longer, is not only incorrect, but it's also a deception that can destroy our lives. I encounter this third deception more frequently than any others—almost on a daily basis—because this definition sounds right to many people.

There is one definition of forgiveness that just won't go away.

I've often had the opportunity to teach a course on developing people-helping skills at a local Bible institute. The purpose of this course is to teach volunteer Christian counselors the necessary information and skills to counsel their friends and family members. Each term, when I begin the section on forgiveness, I ask them to write a definition of what it means to biblically forgive someone.

Then we read their definitions aloud to the class. In every group of students several people write, "Forgiveness is not holding the offender accountable for his wrongdoing—not bringing up the offense to use against him."

When the wife got nervous and sought out an attorney, her husband was not happy.

One of my cases involved a wife who came to me for counseling because her marriage was in trouble. She had a very teachable spirit, eagerly completing all her homework assignments. She also worked hard to implement all the advice I gave her. From time to time, she would ask her husband to join her in our counseling sessions, but he stubbornly refused to come for help. He told her repeatedly that she was the cause of their marital problems, and he was glad to see that she was "finally taking some action to get herself straightened out."

She and I eventually reached the point in the counseling process where it would be nearly impossible to save their marriage unless he agreed to come with her for counseling. As often happens in these kinds of situations, the wife panicked. She spoke with a lawyer who was a member of their church, and asked him to draw up a proposed financial agreement that she and her husband could follow if they should decide to get a divorce. They had three young children and the husband would be required to pay alimony and child support.

When she approached her husband with these facts he suddenly agreed to come to me for counseling. It probably comes as no surprise that he was not smiling when he bulldozed into my office. He was also not very open to receiving help. I noticed he was carrying a yellow legal pad in his hand. I realized that I was face-to-face with "The List Maker."

He began to read his list of offenses, hardly stopping to take a breath.

Faced with the prospect of paying alimony and child support, he had armed himself with a legal pad, 18 pages of which he had filled out in small print. On these pages, he had not listed a single thing he had done to offend, hurt, frustrate, or irritate his wife throughout the years of their marriage. Instead, he had recorded everything he could recall that his wife had *ever* done to offend him. He introduced himself, and sat down on my office sofa. I knew in an instant it was going to be a long hour.

He had recorded every offense his wife had ever committed against him.

He wasted no time, but immediately began to read his list aloud to me. He read, for instance, "January, 14, 1994: She didn't have supper ready for me when I got home. May 4, 1995: House was a mess when I came through the door. Looked like she hadn't done anything all day." This couple had a preschooler, and anyone who has ever had a young child knows how long it takes him to mess up a house—less than 45 seconds. (We have ten kids, and it doesn't even take 45 seconds at our house. In about 15 seconds, our house can look like a tornado hit it.)

I asked if he'd made a list of his offenses against his wife.

Now here was the big one. He had written down every time hiswife had been unresponsive to him sexually. He had listed one date after another, chronicling each time she had resisted his advances. The first time he paused for a good breath, I stopped him and said, "We don't do that kind of counseling here. But I would be interested in hearing the things you've done to hurt your wife."

He ignored my request and immediately proceeded to read his list again. Once more, I stopped him. We repeated this process two or three more times until I realized this man was like a freight train. He intended to move full speed ahead no matter what I said. He was insistent upon reading me his list. So, I finally gave up, put down my pen, sat back in my chair, and determined that I would wait him out until the end of the hour. It was a long hour.

He was indignant when I told him he hadn't forgiven his wife.

About ten minutes before the session was over, I stopped him again. I said, "Based upon the things you've told me today, it's obvious your wife has deeply hurt you." "Well, Dr. Dunlap," he replied with a satisfied expression on his face, "I'm glad to see that you understand where I'm coming from." Then I continued, "It's also clear to me that you've not been willing to forgive your wife for what she's done to offend you."

Well, he was not quite so happy with that comment. He countered indignantly, "I most assuredly have forgiven her. I'm a Christian!" I knew that this man had a graduate degree in psychology from a Christian college, so I asked in dismay, "You honestly believe you've forgiven her?"

He answered, "Yes sir, I certainly do." I continued, "Well, if you've forgiven your wife, would you mind telling me what your definition of forgiveness is?" He sat back in his chair, and I could tell he was thinking hard. After a moment or two a big smile broke across his face and he said, "I think I've got a good definition. Forgiveness is not holding her accountable any longer for what she's done to me."

I recognized his definition for what it was—a deception. I was now certain that "The List Maker" was clueless about biblical forgiveness, and I was grateful to the Lord that this man had agreed to come back for his next appointment.

As I've told the story of "The List Maker" through the years, some people have questioned my response to this guy when he told me his definition of forgiveness: "deciding not to hold an offender accountable any longer." Here's what transpired next.

He had hardly finished speaking when I said loudly, "Wrong!" He jumped back like he'd been hit with a bolt of lightening. This man didn't have a clue about true biblical forgiveness. He was firmly convinced he had done nothing to contribute to the demise of his marriage. He actually believed he was a victim!

The husband told me he had married the wrong person.

When I told him that our first step was to discern God's purposes for allowing his wife to commit these offenses against him, he interrupted me, "I already know what the problem is." "Well what do you think it is?" I asked him. "It's as simple as this," he said. "I married the wrong person." Then I told him, "Sir, marriage does not work that way. You stood in the presence of God and witnesses and exchanged your wedding vows.

If you had any doubts before about God's 'right' person for your life, your vows permanently settled that question." I continued, "The only thing that could ever undo your vows is if your wife were to get involved in ongoing adultery and refuse to repent—and she's not doing that—or if she were unwilling to fulfill the most basic responsibilities associated with marriage and she deserted you." (I knew that didn't apply to this marriage either.)

His parents pressured their son to come for marriage counseling.

Still he held out, stubbornly refusing to open his heart or his mind to any possible good that God could bring out of his wife's offenses towards him. Men who maintain this sort of attitude usually don't come back after the first or second appointment. However, this man kept coming back week after week.

Later I found out from his wife the reason why. He was in business with his parents who were committed Christians. When they heard that he was considering divorce, they asked him to come to me for counseling because they were supporting their son in the business. They knew they would be paying the bulk of the alimony and child support if a divorce happened. You might say they had exerted a little parental pressure on him.

After several weeks, we came to the application point in the counseling process. He had to decide what he was going to do. I reminded him that when we began meeting together several weeks earlier, he had wrongly assumed he had forgiven his wife because he had made a choice not to hold her accountable any longer for her offenses. Then once again, I earnestly urged him to implement the principles he had learned and biblically forgive his wife.

He continued to blame his wife for all their marital problems.

On the one hand, we had the 18 pages of offenses he had recorded. On the other hand, we had the biblical principles of forgiveness, and the steps he needed to take to forgive his wife. I asked him if he was ready to choose to forgive her for everything. He looked at his two choices that afternoon and replied, "I firmly believe that if my wife would get her attitude straightened out we could do fine in this relationship." He then made a decision not to forgive her, and three months later he divorced her.

Chapter 5

What Does "Forgive and Forget" Mean?

Forgiveness Deception #4: God commands us to forgive and forget.

Learning to forgive biblically involves learning to respond correctly to *God* when people offend us. Nowhere in the Bible are we commanded to forgive and forget. In fact, painful memories can be an excellent motivation to praise God. Memories of getting through trials victoriously provide us with a reservoir of praise and thanksgiving. We recognize how God used those trials to make us more like Jesus. So our goal in learning to forgive, therefore, is not to forget, but to remember in the right way.

This fourth deception is pervasive—many Christians have wholeheartedly embraced it. They adamantly believe that to forgive is to forget. I've encountered this definition countless times. I've heard it on Christian radio. I've read it in magazine articles. There's even a book entitled "Forgive and Forget."

The basic premise of the "Forgive and Forget" supposition is this: If offended people truly forgive their offender, they will eventually arrive at a point where they no longer have any conscious recollection of the offense. In a word, the offense will "fade" from memory.

While this sounds very pious, the truth of the matter is that nowhere in the Bible does God command us to forgive and forget. We don't usually have the ability to forget. We may, of course, forget small, inconsequential things, but we don't easily forget the big things. Forgiveness does, however, involve learning how to remember in the right way.

My wife and I experienced intense conflict in the early years of our marriage. Although they took place over twenty years ago, I still remember some of those angry encounters as if they happened yesterday. Our arguments usually followed a predictable path. I would selfishly clam up and use the silent treatment to punish her for her angry outbursts. We quickly reached an impasse in communication with one another. My immaturity and her anger brought us to the point of divorce.

Allow painful memories to become a reminder to praise God.

In His mercy, God led us to a Christian counselor who taught us how to implement the steps of biblical forgiveness in our marriage. My wife and I can attest to the fact that the memories of those days are no longer negative. Instead, those memories provide us with a reservoir of praise and thanksgiving that we offer to God every time we think of those early years. We recognize how He used the trials of those difficult years to change us and to make us more like Jesus Christ.

Chapter 6

Holding an Offender Accountable

Forgiveness Deception #5: An offended person has the right to hold the offender personally accountable for the wrong he committed.

In biblical forgiveness, an offended person has no right to hold the offender personally accountable for his wrongdoing. In this chapter, we'll explore the effects of this fifth deception, through the case study of a rebellious teenage girl. Molested as a child, this adolescent was untrustworthy, violent toward her own family, and thoroughly incorrigible.

The girl wouldn't look me in the eye, and she wouldn't say a word.

This case study began several years ago when a husband and wife brought their 15-year-old daughter to me for counseling. She was one of the most rebellious teenagers I had ever met. She was into the "grunge" look. If you're not familiar with "grunge," it was a counter-culture clothing fad several years ago. Grunge fans looked like they had just crawled out of a garbage can.

This young girl had an earring in her nose, several earrings in both ears and blond-streaked hair that was matted down on her head. Her hair came down over her eyes, so she didn't have to look directly at anyone unless she chose to. She did not choose to look at me.

When her parents left her in charge of her younger brother, she would beat him up.

She had been sneaking out of her bedroom window each night to be with her friends. This was a special challenge because she lived in a second-story bedroom. She had one sibling—a 13-year old brother. Her parents were afraid to leave her alone with him because, if she and her brother got into an argument, she would beat him up.

The family attended an evangelical, Bible-believing church. The Youth Pastor had informed the parents that he could no longer allow their daughter to attend youth functions. She was so rebellious and disruptive she made it impossible for him to carry out the regular youth activities. He went on to say she was welcome at church only if she agreed to sit beside her parents. No one wanted to be around her. Her parents told me the dog didn't even like her.

Her grandfather had sexually molested her for seven years.

The first time her father brought her to me for counseling, he left her in the waiting room with her mother. He filled me in on her background and ended with, "One other thing that you need to know about our daughter is that from the time she was 4 years old until she was 11, she was sexually molested by her paternal grandfather."

This grandfather was a deacon in his church; a prominent member of the community; and very wealthy. He used his money as a means to continue his molestation for those seven years. He would bribe her with gifts and cash. She knew if she ever told anyone what was going on, she would no longer receive all the things he gave her. For years, he used the material perks to control and manipulate her.

Then her school presented a sex-education program when she was in fifth grade. She watched a video entitled "Good Touch, Bad Touch." Her teacher instructed all the students, "If you've ever been touched in a 'bad touch' way, you need to tell someone today."

She finally had the courage to tell her parents about the sexual abuse.

That afternoon when she got home from school, she mustered up all her courage because she was about to do the hardest thing she had ever done in all her life. She told her mother what had been happening. As soon as her father came home that evening, her mother assessed him of the situation. His initial response, though not at all uncommon, was dead wrong. The story of this teenage girl's life is one of the most glorious accounts of God's healing power that I have ever witnessed. God worked miraculously to restore wholeness and beauty to a broken, fragmented life.

Her parents told her she could never again bring up the topic of her sexual abuse.

Later that evening the mother went to this girl and said, "We're never going to talk about this again." They dropped her accusation like a hot potato. During the next two years, this teenager began to develop rebellious attitudes, and she began to migrate to other kids who shared her negative outlook because she felt accepted by them.

When she was 13 years old, school officials told her parents, "We don't know what your daughter's problem is, but she's on the fast track to becoming a drop-out." They informed the parents that the school would not allow her to re-enroll for the next school term unless she received professional counseling.

She told her story to four professional counselors over the next two years.

In an effort to be good, conscientious Christian parents, they took her to see a psychologist. For two years, she saw four different men—two psychologists and two psychiatrists. Then when she was 15, her parents heard her throwing up in the bathroom. They suspected that she had an eating disorder. They brought her to the physician I worked with at the time for a physical examination. After examining her, he immediately referred the entire family to me.

Soon the two of us were sitting face to face in my office. The first thing I told her was if she had any hope whatsoever of leading a normal life, she would have to be willing to forgive her grandfather. I told her she would also have to be willing to forgive her parents. She wouldn't talk to me. I couldn't blame her.

I think that if I'd been required to repeat this sordid tale again and again to four different counselors, I wouldn't have been in much of a talkative mood either. Therefore, I didn't try to get her to talk. Instead, I began to gradually set before her the biblical principles of forgiveness.

She believed her grandfather had gotten away with his wicked behavior.

When I presented the principle that we do not have the right to hold our offenders accountable for their wrongdoings, I could almost hear her screaming on the inside. As far as she was concerned, her grandfather had gotten away with his evil deeds. Six months earlier one of the psychiatrists she was seeing had telephoned her grandfather and confronted him with her accusation.

She was sitting there in his office when this call took place. The grandfather vehemently denied ever having touched her and then asked the psychiatrist sarcastically, "Have you taken one good look at my granddaughter?" He was right. If he and his granddaughter had ever ended up in court, his being convicted, based upon her testimony, would have been very unlikely. She was angry, rebellious and hostile. She didn't appear to be a very credible witness. The grandfather ended the conversation by telling the psychiatrist, "If you ever call me again be prepared to talk to my attorney."

When the psychiatrist told her what her grandfather had said, his words drove her feelings of hatred and despair deeper into her heart. She gave up any hope of ever seeing justice in this matter, and she made up her mind to live behind her shell of bitterness and rebellion.

Most of us experienced a similar kind of disgust when the O.J. Simpson trial was being conducted. Despite the fact that he denied his guilt and was acquitted of the crime, two people were killed, and there is still a murderer walking the streets of Southern California or elsewhere. We wanted to see justice prevail for the people who died, but there has been no justice.

I told her God holds us accountable for every thought, word and action.

This 15-year old girl believed her grandfather had gotten away with his crime against her, and her heart was being consumed by a desire for revenge. She desperately needed to hear the principles of biblical forgiveness. First, I shared with her the scriptural principle that God holds us accountable for every thought, every word, and every deed.

Then I explained that God designed a place where sin would be paid for—on the cross where Jesus took upon Himself God's penalty of wrath for the sins of all the redeemed in years past, in the present and in years to come. I went on to tell her that sin will be accounted for on Judgment Day at the end of time.

God deals with sin while we're on this earth.

However, the truth she needed most to hear at that moment was that God deals with sin right here on earth, right now. This girl needed to grasp the truth that her grandfather had not gotten away with one single vile offense he had committed against her during that seven-year period.

I told her about the reaping and sowing principle, and I showed her Galatians 6:7, "Do not be deceived, God is not mocked; for whatever a man sows, this he will also reap." She had been deceived. She thought her grandfather had gotten away with his sin. God is not mocked. What that man did to that young girl was mockery in the sight of God.

We sometimes deal with difficult relationships in our lives. Perhaps it's a work associate or a boss. Maybe it's a husband or a wife. For parents, it could be a rebellious teenager. We can be assured they won't get away with their harsh, selfish, disrespectful attitudes. God tells us in His Word, "Whatever a man sows, that he will also reap." This principle is as certain as the rising and setting of the sun.

I told her God was going to get her grandfather in His perfect timing.

Then I shared 2 Thessalonians 1:6 with this young girl, "It is only just for God to repay with affliction those who afflict you." God is going to get evildoers. She needed to know that. She needed to know that as long as her grandfather lived on this earth in an unrepentant state, he would never experience genuine joy or peace. He would never enjoy God's hand of blessing upon his life.

I told her, "Your grandfather may still have his money, but if he doesn't acknowledge God as the source of his wealth, his money will be a curse to him. The fact that he finds his security in materialism is the very thing that will most likely keep him from repentance." She needed to understand that as well.

However, there was yet one very important principle that she needed to comprehend before she would be ready to biblically forgive her grandfather.

Our sinful hearts need a frequent reminder of the warning in Proverbs 24:17,18: "Do not gloat when your enemy falls; and do not let your heart rejoice when he stumbles, lest the Lord see it and be displeased, and He will turn away His anger from him."

We must take care not to rejoice when our enemy falls. If any of us were to get what we deserve, we would have no hope for the eternal security of our souls. Our fallen race is deserving of hell. Apart from the perfect blood of Jesus Christ, we could never pay God the debt we owe for our willful rebellion against His holiness and our flagrant transgression of His law.

At last she began to look me in the eye and communicate.

The teenage girl, who had been sexually abused for years by her unrepentant grandfather, slowly began to grasp the truths of biblical forgiveness. I saw a marked change in her countenance. She began to look me in the eye. She began to communicate with me.

As we considered the principles of forgiveness over a period of several weeks, she began to have hope for the first time. She did not like the person she had become, and she knew that no one else liked her either.

The time soon arrived in the counseling process when she had to make a life-changing decision. On the one hand, we had the list of all the offenses her grandfather had committed against her. On the other hand, we had the principles of biblical forgiveness that would set her free from the resentment, the anger, and the bitterness that had controlled her life for four years.

She didn't have any feelings of forgiveness for her grandfather.

When the moment arrived for her to apply the truths of forgiveness she hesitated. "I don't have any feelings of forgiveness towards him," she told me. She thought she was supposed to have tender emotions in her heart before she could forgive him. I explained that forgiveness is an act of our will—something we choose to do.

In cases such as this, *feelings* of forgiveness hardly ever precede the *act* of forgiveness. I told her that the first step she needed to take was to consciously and deliberately forgive her grandfather before God. I assured her that her feelings would become more balanced as the Lord granted her grace in response to her obedience to Him.

Her life became a source of encouragement to other young women.

The transformation that occurred in her life, thereafter, was dramatic. By the time she graduated high school, she was one of the most committed Christians in her church youth group. She shared her testimony at a school assembly that was sponsored by Fellowship of Christian Athletes. She stood before hundreds of her peers and explained the change that had taken place in her life. She described how God had enabled her to forgive the man who had sexually abused her for seven years.

Soon, other young girls began to stop her in the halls at school and tell her they had been through similar experiences. Each time a girl indicated a willingness to seek help she would bring her to me for counseling. Her life testimony became a beautiful source of encouragement to countless lives.

Statistics reveal that one in every four women experiences some form of sexual abuse. One in every six men suffers sexual abuse. The principles of biblical forgiveness have the power to set hurting people free.

Chapter 7

When to Say "I Forgive You"

Forgiveness Deception #6: When we forgive an offender before God, we must then go to the offender and tell him, "I forgive you."

This is a very common misconception, and one that I frequently hear in my counseling appointments. But God hasn't authorized us to do this for our offenders. The truth is, we grant forgiveness to an offender only when he repents and asks for our forgiveness.

He wrote a letter to his father that made matters worse.

Recently a man who had been going to a psychologist for three years came to me for counseling. After counseling this man for a few weeks, the psychologist had instructed him to write a letter to his father and confront him for all the ways he had offended him when he was growing up.

The man told me, "I wrote that letter to my father. It was five pages long. In the final paragraph, I expressed to my father that I had forgiven him for all the horrible things he did to me when I was a kid." There had been a lot of anger and conflict in his family. He said, "Dr. Dunlap, it's been almost three years since I wrote my father that letter, and I haven't heard from him to this day." That didn't surprise me at all. This man had dealt with his father's offenses in the wrong way.

She asked me if she should tell her grandfather she had forgiven him.

Several months after I completed the counseling process with the 15-year-old girl who had been sexually molested by her grandfather, she phoned me one day with a question. She asked if she should approach her grandfather at an upcoming family reunion to tell him she had forgiven him.

I explained to her that while we're biblically obligated to forgive our offender before God, whether or not he repents, we grant forgiveness to an offender only when he repents and asks for it. Jesus tells us in Luke 17, "If your brother offends you seven times a day, and seven times a day he comes to you and says, 'I repent,' forgive him." I told her she could not tell her grandfather she forgave him. God doesn't authorize us to do that for our offenders. Her grandfather had never even acknowledged the fact that he had done anything wrong.

If she had sought him out to tell him she forgave him, he would either have been infuriated at her suggestion of his guilt, or he would have thought, "Well, I'm off the hook now. She's forgiven me." And he certainly was *not* off the hook. He was not off the hook with God, first and foremost, and he was not off the hook legally.

God tells us we must treat our enemies with kindness.

Most counselors I know would have told her, "Don't ever see your grandfather again. Avoid any family gatherings that you think he might attend. If he arrives unexpectedly at a gathering, leave immediately. Never again put yourself in a position to interact with him." However, is that the biblical approach?

Scripture gives us very specific guidelines for how we're to treat our enemies. Jesus tells us in "The Sermon on the Mount" to love our enemies and to pray for them. The writer of Romans 12 instructs us to feed our enemies if they are hungry, and to give them something to drink if they're thirsty.

So we worked out a strategy for how she should greet her grandfather each time she encountered him. Her parents were always to be at her side. When she approached him, she was to extend her hand to greet him courteously and respectfully.

She had a great time at the family reunion. She was able, for the first time in years, to relate to her grandfather without bitterness and resentment in her heart. Everyone was amazed at the transformation that had taken place in her life.

Chapter 8

The Wife Who Demanded Respect

Forgiveness Deception #8: I have the right to act sullen and hurt when someone offends me.

Acting sullen after you've been offended, in order to teach your offender a lesson, is unbiblical. People who behave this way, generally, hope the offender will learn his lesson and won't make the mistake again of violating their rights. Something innate in the heart of a sinful man seems naturally to respond to offenses in this manner.

This next case study involves a woman who had checked into a private psychiatric ward because she was experiencing depression. In most psychiatric facilities, group counseling is the method of choice. The first night she was there, the doctor on call placed her in a group of about nine or ten women. The group was moderated by a social worker, and the woman was expected to express her problems to the entire group.

She confided in them that she was depressed because of her marriage situation. She told the women her husband was insensitive, uncommunicative and ungrateful. She had tried to maintain a good relationship with him. She had even been willing to go to counseling, but her husband refused to go with her. Basically, she believed she was doing most of the giving in their marriage, and he was doing most of the taking.

They told her it was time for her to draw up some guidelines in her marriage.

Before the session was over all the women in the group came down hard on this new member. They told her she had become co-dependent. This is a very popular word in modern psychology. They told her when a woman allows a man to take advantage of her, he does exactly that. They warned her to establish boundaries in the relationship. Then, they advised her to demand to be treated with respect, dignity, and consideration.

All of this sounded pretty good to her. She had tried the nagging and complaining approach, and it hadn't worked. She thought perhaps she had finally found the missing ingredient that would make this marriage work. After a ten-day stay in the psychiatric facility (where she ran up a bill of more than $10,000), she was released to go home. She took a little notebook home with her that outlined exactly how she was to talk with her husband.

She told her husband she wanted to have a meeting with him.

The first thing she was supposed to do was call a family meeting. That's not a bad idea. I frequently recommend that sort of thing. However, her assignment was to tell her husband how they were going to restructure their relationship based upon mutual consideration, kindness, self-sacrifice, and communication.

The ladies in the group had suggested that this husband and wife meet together each evening after the dinner meal for 30 minutes and talk about three things that had happened to them that day. Then they were supposed to talk about how they each felt about those three things. That's not a bad idea either, and it would have been an excellent suggestion if it had been made under different circumstances.

This husband, however, didn't appreciate his wife giving him a list of demands. Three weeks later, the physician I worked with got a call from the emergency room at the hospital. The wife had tried to commit suicide. If she had been discovered half an hour later, she would have been dead. She wasn't merely trying to get her husband's attention. She had actually tried to take her life. I was thankful for the opportunity to meet with her. And I was thankful for the principles of biblical forgiveness, which I knew could change her life.

She had deeply resented her husband for years.

When her psychiatrist released her from the psychiatric ward, he sent her to her family physician, who then referred her to me for counseling. I quickly perceived that she was deeply resentful towards her husband, so we began to review the principles of biblical forgiveness. It soon became clear to me that she had harbored feelings of anger and hurt toward him for years.

I commonly encounter counselees who have been bitter and resentful for decades. Whether a person's conflict is with a neighbor, a work associate, or a marriage partner, if he continues to nurse his wounded emotions, he can be certain he doesn't have God's perspective in the matter. Furthermore, he hasn't responded properly yet to the situation.

I asked her to fill out a list of 110 things wives do to destroy their marriage.

The first thing I asked this wife to do was a homework assignment. She was to take home a list I developed which includes 110 things wives do to hurt, frustrate, irritate, and offend their husbands. I told her, "For the next seven days, don't think about any of the things your husband has done to offend you. Instead, I want you to come before God with this list and ask him to reveal to you all the things you've done to contribute to your marriage problems."

God's Word reassures us, "Neither God nor man despise a broken, contrite, humble spirit." I told her that after she had gone through this checklist I wanted her to write out all her offenses in detail, as preparation for asking for her husband's forgiveness for each offense. I encouraged her to be very thorough in this exercise. I have never seen a counselee write too much when he goes through this list. The problem is that some counselees don't write enough. They flippantly gloss over their sins, and their repentance is incomplete and insincere.

When she came back the next week she seemed to be transformed.

She returned for her appointment the following week with a vastly different attitude. The Holy Spirit had begun to convict her heart, and she was humbled. Her husband was still living in their home, but he was marking time, waiting for an apartment to come available. Although I had no idea whether or not he would be responsive, I advised her to phone her husband and invite him to meet with us.

She called him at work and said, "I know that the last time I asked you to meet with me our talk didn't go well. I will understand if you choose not to meet with me again, but I want you to know that God has convicted me of how wrong my attitudes and actions toward you have been. I've asked the Lord to forgive me, and I would be very grateful if you'd give me the opportunity to sit down with you one last time to ask you to forgive me for what I've done." He agreed to meet with her, and God began a healing process in their relationship that eventually led to their reconciliation.

She wept tears of repentance as she asked her husband to forgive her.

She had not been preparing meals for him for quite some time, but she made dinner for him that evening. As they sat down to eat their meal, she began to go over her list. It took her two hours. Her list wasn't that long. While it's true that she had accumulated quite a number of offenses during their many years of marriage, it was her grief and weeping over her offenses that significantly prolonged the repentance process.

Her husband showed up in my office the very next week. He had never before been willing to go to anyone for counseling, but he was impressed by the humility he had witnessed in his wife's life. For the first time, he had hope that their marriage could be saved. I met with them weekly, for three months.

They were both willing to humble themselves before God and one another. They sought each other's forgiveness, and they implemented the principles of biblical forgiveness in their relationship. Because of their obedience to God's commands, and because of the Lord's powerful, healing grace, their marriage was restored.

Chapter 9

Focus On the Offense, Not the Offender

Forgiveness Principle #1: When you've been offended, you must readjust your focus from a negative view of the offender, to a positive view of the offense.

Forgiveness is usually not something that happens instantaneously. It is a process that develops over a period of time. There are ten Forgiveness Principles that are worthy of consideration for anyone who wants to learn how to begin forgiving others biblically.

Romans 8:28 and James 1:2-4 are helpful scripture verses for someone who is learning to apply this principle of forgiveness. Most Christians can quote Romans 8:28 almost as easily as they can quote John 3:16. I have even met many unsaved people who know Romans 8:28: "We know that God causes all things to work together for good to those who love God, to those who are called according to His purpose."

There are two words in this verse that merit a closer examination. The first word is "know." This is a very strong word in the Greek language. It is a knowledge that is based upon certain verifiable facts. It is a *knowing* that is *certain* because it is rooted in the integrity and righteousness of God. The second key word is "all." Is it true that God works in *all* circumstances for the benefit of His children?

Romans 8:28 is true all the time, for all Christians, everywhere.

I often ask my counselees if they truly believe Romans 8:28. Most of them are professing Christians and they answer "yes." When I ask them why they believe this verse, they usually tell me that God's Word says it's true, so they believe it. Then I give them another reason to believe it's true. I tell them that in the last 20 years, I have observed something very encouraging in the approximately 25,000 counseling sessions I've conducted. When counselees have chosen to apply the principles of biblical forgiveness to their various problems, God has brought wondrous good out of the most horrible situations imaginable—in every single instance, without exception. God never fails to keep His promises to His children.

God desires to build the character of Jesus into our lives and He uses our trials and hardships to accomplish that goal.

Why does a loving God allow His children to endure trials and heartaches in life? God wants to build the very character of His Son into our lives, and He uses the difficulties we face as a primary means with to do that. God may choose to sacrifice our marriage, our friendships, our financial security, or our health. The Lord resists us when we demonstrate stubbornness and pride, but He grants us grace when we humble ourselves before Him.

Having considered the promise of Romans 8:28, we now turn our attention to the command of James 1:2, "Count it all joy my brothers whenever you face trials of many kinds." The phrase, "trials of many kinds," is used several times in the New Testament. We encounter two basic kinds of trials in our lives. One kind is the trial of our own making. If someone hits my car when I willfully run a red light, I must face a hardship that I brought upon myself.

Christians aren't immune to the trials and heartaches of life.

The second type of trial is any difficult situation we must face that is beyond our control. These are trials we had no part in causing. When Hurricane Andrew ripped its devastating path through Miami, it didn't jump over the Methodists, and hit the Baptists and the Presbyterians. It indiscriminately destroyed whatever homes happened to be in its path. God tells us in His Word that the rain falls on the just and the unjust. It's quite *unlikely* that those homes were destroyed because of the homeowners' sin.

When the going gets tough, never give up.

The writer of James 1:3 goes on to say that the testing of our faith produces perseverance in our character. To persevere is to do what is right in the midst of difficult circumstances, and to continue to do what's right even though the circumstances may not change. In James 1:4 we read that perseverance must finish its work so that we may be mature and complete, not lacking anything. What does a mature and complete person look like? We find the answer in Philippians 2:5: "Have the same attitudes in yourself which were also in Christ Jesus."

As I mentioned previously, my wife and I experienced some extremely rocky years early in our marriage. We nearly divorced before I was willing to ask someone for help. I held graduate degrees in counseling, education, and theology, and I believed I knew all there was to know about fixing troubled marriages. I thought, "I ought to be able to figure this problem out by myself. I understand the Bible, and I'm reasonably intelligent."

However, all I really had was a lot of knowledge and very little wisdom. God's Word tells us that knowledge "puffs a man up." I also had a large dose of pride that nearly destroyed our marriage. We read this warning in James 4:6: "God resists the proud but He gives grace to the humble."

God will sacrifice anything in our lives to make us more like Jesus Christ.

In order to accomplish His purpose in us, God may sacrifice our marriage, our friendships, our financial security, or our health. He may even allow our children to be afflicted. God uses all these situations to get our attention. Most Christians possess varying degrees of stubbornness and pride. And we're unlikely to develop Christ-like attitudes unless we're under pressure. So God lovingly enrolls us in the school of "various trials" to give us opportunities to grow to be more like Him.

God does whatever's necessary in our lives to prepare us for eternity.

The story of Job shows us the correct attitude to have toward life's trials, and the great rewards of such an attitude. We shouldn't be surprised that God will sacrifice anything in our lives to prepare us to live with Him eternally.

A book in the Old Testament provides us with a blueprint for facing trials in a way that honors God. Job dealt with his trials in an exemplary way. He was a righteous man—his problems didn't come upon him because of sin in his life. He suffered horrible physical affliction. Painful boils covered his body from the top of his head to the bottom of his feet, he couldn't sit or lie down, and he experienced agonizing, relentless pain.

Job lost everything he cherished and almost everyone he loved.

Job was a family man who had immense wealth. He owned thousands of animals and vast amounts of real estate. He was unquestionably financially secure. Then his enemies stole all his possessions, and a whirlwind killed his ten children while they were feasting together in one place. Job was overcome with grief.But his friends didn't understand much about trusting God in the midst of trials.

His friends came to "encourage" him with a few suggestions.

Job's friends told him he was going through all his problems because he had sin in his life. His wife told him to curse God and die. Yet Job's answer reveals the strength of his character and the depth of his commitment to the Lord: "Shall we indeed accept good from God and not accept adversity?" Job understood the secret of contentment.

We can't take our material possessions to heaven with us. In heaven, these frail bodies of dust will no longer encumber us. We'll be given flawless bodies that are not feeble or sickly. We can't take our spouse with us because the Bible tells us there will be no marriage in heaven. We can't take our children with us, although we pray that our Christian testimony will be a righteous influence in their lives.

People and the Word of God are all that will last into eternity.

Only two things are going to pass through the veil from this life into the life to come. The human soul will live forever in either heaven or hell, and the Word of God will live for all eternity. The writer of Isaiah 40:7 tells us: "The grass withers and the flowers fade, but the Word of our God stands forever."

God does whatever is necessary in our lives to prepare us for eternity.

We shouldn't be surprised at the fact that God will sacrifice anything in our lives—our health, our financial security, our job, our marriage, our children, our friends or our church—in order to prepare us for those things that last for eternity. He prepares our soul to live with Him eternally.

☐

A counselee once reacted strongly to my suggestion that God, in His wisdom, would allow her marriage to fall apart because He desired to accomplish something specific in her character. "Don't you know what the Bible has to say about divorce?" she challenged me. "Yes," I answered, "but we also read, for instance, in 1 Corinthians 3:16 that our body is a temple of the Holy Spirit and God dwells in us.

You recall that 11 of the 12 disciples died a martyrs' death. Their bodies were sacred dwelling places for God's spirit on earth, but God allowed them to be destroyed because He wanted to accomplish His purpose in their deaths—to spread the Gospel of Jesus Christ throughout the world." "Yes," I concluded, "I believe that God would even sacrifice your marriage in order to prepare you for eternity."

Chapter 10

Our Offenders—God's Instruments

Forgiveness Principle #2: We should view our offender as an instrument of God in our lives.

Many people don't readily agree with this principle. Some have commented, "If you said offenders are instruments of the devil, I could understand that, but it almost sounds heretical to imply that someone who committed an offense against me is an instrument of God. How could this be true?"

Let's take a look at the Old Testament patriarch, Joseph. His life provides one of the greatest examples in Scripture of biblical forgiveness. We learned in Forgiveness Principle #1 that when we're offended we must readjust our focus from a negative view of the offender, to a positive view of the offense. In this second forgiveness principle, we learn why we ought to perceive our offenders positively.

Joseph was one of Jacob's sons, and his father loved him more than he loved his other children. He gave Joseph a beautiful multi-colored coat that became a visual reminder to his brothers of his favored status. All of his brothers were jealous of him.

When he was 17 years old, he told his brothers about two of his dreams. He dreamed that 11 sheaves of wheat were bowing down to his sheaf, and that the sun, the moon, and 11 stars were also bowing down to him. His brothers grew even angrier with him and asked, "Are you, the youngest brother, actually going to rule over us?"

Joseph's own brothers planned to murder him.

One day, his father sent him out to the pasture to check on his brothers who were tending their flocks. As they saw him walking toward them in his beautiful coat, they gave in to their hatred and plotted to kill him. Had it not been for the oldest brother Reuben's intervention, they would have murdered Joseph. Instead, they stripped him of his coveted coat and threw him into a pit.

⬜

His brothers cruelly sold him into slavery and then lied to their father.

When one of the brothers spotted a caravan of Egyptian traders approaching, he suggested that they sell Joseph into slavery. The plan seemed ingenious. They wouldn't have to live with the guilt of murdering their brother, they would pick up a little pocket change, and they would rid themselves of the problem that had plagued their lives for 17 years. They tore up the coat, dipped it in goat's blood, and returned it to their father, explaining that a wild beast had devoured Joseph.

Joseph was now on his way to Egypt. In Egypt, a high government official named Potiphar, who was part of Pharaoh's royal guard, bought Joseph. God blessed him while he served under Potiphar and everything he did prospered. Potiphar, being a wise and prudent man, soon made Joseph the administrator of his entire household.

Joseph ran from temptation and was rewarded with a prison sentence.

Everything went well until Potiphar's wife noticed that Joseph was, as the Bible describes him, a handsome young Israelite. When she tried to seduce him, he fled from her presence. As he fled, she grabbed his outer garment as evidence that she had been with him, and then she accused Joseph of sexually attacking her. The penalty for such a crime, in most cases, would have been death. Potiphar, however, may have had some doubt as to his wife's credibility, and instead he placed Joseph in Pharaoh's prison.

Sometime later, when Pharaoh became furious at his chief cupbearer and his chief baker, he imprisoned them along with Joseph. Both of these men had dreams and Joseph interpreted them. He accurately foretold that the baker would be executed in three days. He told the cupbearer, however, that he would be restored to his former position.

Once Joseph's fellow prisoner was released from jail, he forgot about Joseph's kindness.

Joseph then asked a personal favor of the cupbearer. He explained that he had been imprisoned unjustly. Joseph asked the cupbearer to mentiion on his name to Pharaoh, in hopes that he might be released. However as often happens when someone escapes dire circumstances, the cupbearer forgot about his friend who had helped to deliver him. Once he was reinstated to his former job the cupbearer made no mention of Joseph to Pharaoh.

Joseph won Pharaoh's confidence by accurately interpreting his dreams. In time, Pharaoh himself had two strange dreams. He dreamed that seven thin cows ate seven fat cows, and seven thin ears of grain ate seven plump ears of grain. The dreams tormented Pharaoh, and he sent for all the dream interpreters throughout the land of Egypt. When no one could interpret Pharaoh's dreams, the cupbearer remembered Joseph, who then described to Pharaoh the coming years of plenty and of famine.

He explained the need to prepare for the impending famine by organizing a food storage plan. Pharaoh was so grateful to Joseph for interpreting his dreams that he appointed him second in command over the entire land of Egypt.

When the famine finally began, ten of Joseph's brothers traveled to Egypt to buy food so that their family would not starve. They didn't recognize Joseph, and they certainly never suspected that their brother would be the second most powerful man in all of Egypt.

Joseph's brothers were terrified that he would retaliate against them.

When Joseph at last revealed his identity to his brothers, he told them not to be distressed. But they had good reason to be *very* distressed. They had threatened to kill Joseph, and they had sold him into a life of slavery. He now stood before them with the power to execute them all. Joseph continued, "Don't be angry with yourselves." Anyone who has ever been angry with himself or herself for doing something unwise can surely identify with Joseph's brothers at this point in the narrative.

Then Joseph told them something amazing: "What you intended for evil, God used for good." This is an example of the principle of God's sovereignty that is found throughout the Old and New Testaments. God promises us, from Genesis to Revelation, that when other people intend to hurt us or make our lives difficult, He uses those things for our good.

The need to forgive our offenders is emphasized throughout Scripture.

The theme of forgiveness appears in almost every story in the Old Testament. Throughout His Word, God reassures us that He is in control of every detail of our lives. No evil can touch us unless He first allows it. We can be certain He will use every trial that befalls us, to conform us more completely to the image of His Son Jesus Christ.

The Old Testament story of Balaam provides an interesting illustration of forgiveness.

When someone offends us, we naturally tend to focus on who the offender is, and on what he has done to hurt us. If we desire to reap spiritual benefits from our offenses, however, we must understand this principle of forgiveness: God lovingly uses our offenders as instruments of grace to achieve His righteous purposes in our lives.

We find a compelling illustration of forgiveness in the Old Testament story of Balaam. God had finally given the children of Israel permission to cease from their wandering in the Sinai Desert. The time had come for them to enter the Promised Land.

The Israelites had conquered every army that they encountered on their way to the Promised Land. As they approached the eastern side of the Dead Sea they prepared to face their final enemy—the army from the land of Moab.

Balak, the king of Moab, was alarmed when he got word that the Israelites were approaching his country.

The king of Moab heard the Israelites were coming. He knew they were the victors in every battle they had fought. When he found out a certain prophet named Balaam could perform wondrous signs and miracles, he sent for him.

God warned Balaam in a dream not to go to Moab, but the Moabite king was persistent. He offered Balaam great sums of money to come and curse the Israelites so the Moabite army could defeat them in battle. Balaam finally decided that he would go and hear what the king had to say.

Balaam didn't understand that God was using his donkey as an instrument to save his life.

He saddled his donkey for the day and a half journey to the king's castle. As Balaam was traveling on his way, the animal stopped in the middle of the road. In frustration Balaam began to beat his donkey, but he wouldn't move another inch. The donkey's stubbornness and disobedience greatly angered Balaam.

What he didn't know was that God had supernaturally opened the donkey's eyes. The animal saw that directly in front of him stood an angel of the Lord with a flaming sword in his hand. Then God permitted the donkey to speak. He turned to Balaam and asked, "Why are you treating me this way? Am I not your faithful donkey on which you have ridden all your life?"

When Balaam saw how God was using his animal he repented of his anger.

The prophet became very upset when his donkey began speaking to him. Then God also gave Balaam the supernatural ability to see the angel with the flaming sword. When Balaam realized that the angel would have killed him had it not been for his donkey's obedience, he fell on his face and repented of his sin.

God wants us to understand that He uses our offenders mightily in our lives.

When someone offends us, we naturally tend to focus on who the offender is and on what he has done to hurt us. However, if we want to reap spiritual benefit from our offenses, we must understand this principle of forgiveness: God lovingly uses our offenders as instruments of grace to achieve His righteous purposes in our lives.

Judas, for example, was one of the key instruments that God used to send His Son to Calvary. The Lord may use an unfaithful husband, an angry wife, or a rebellious teenager to accomplish something in our lives that could not have been accomplished in any other way. When we understand this principle of biblical forgiveness, we begin to view our offenders from God's perspective. God used a donkey in Balaam's life and He can use any instrument He chooses in our lives—to sanctify us and to make us more like His beloved Son, Jesus Christ.

Chapter 11

Vengeance Is God's—Not Ours

What does it mean to "heap burning coals on our enemies?

What does God think about our taking revenge on our offenders? It is not sinful to have hurt feelings. But we must find out what God instructs us to do with our hurt feelings, and we should remember never to repay anyone with evil. God doesn't permit His children to "get even" with their offenders. He has a more excellent plan.

It's normal to feel hurt when someone offends us. We're not robots. God created us with emotions and we inevitably feel hurt when offenses occur. But our goal, as Believers, is to learn what God expects us to *do* with our hurt feelings. We have to process those feelings realistically and deal with them biblically. Above all, we need to acknowledge Romans 12:17 as our guiding principle when we're offended: "Do not repay anyone evil for evil." This truth is stated in the third forgiveness principle.

Forgiveness Principle #3: When we choose to maintain hurt feelings against an offender we exercise a form of vengeance--called "getting back" at someone. But God does not permit His children to take their own revenge.

In our family we regularly teach the Romans 12:17 command, "not to repay evil for evil." When one of our children, for example, hits, bites, pinches, scratches, shoves, spits on or kicks a sibling, and the offended party responds by hitting, biting, pinching, scratching, shoving, spitting or kicking, the child who returned evil for evil receives the heavier penalty. Without exception, we discipline both offenders swiftly and firmly, but the child who struck back in retaliation receives a double portion.

My wife and I strive to teach our children, from the time they're very young, how to deal successfully with conflict. We want them to learn that a reaction to an offense is as wrong in God's sight as the offense itself. We've found that it takes about 18 years to teach a child this principle. When our hearts are equipped with this truth, however, we understand how to respond rightly to any conflict we

□

encounter in life.

God doesn't allow His children to "get even" with one another.

God instructs us to live at peace with everyone *as far as it depends on us.* There are, admittedly, times in our lives when living peacefully with someone is beyond our control. The Lord wants us to leave room in such situations for His wrath to be administered. He has forbidden us to take our own revenge against an offender. He promises in Romans 12:19, "It is mine to avenge. I will repay."

What does it really mean to "heap burning coals" on someone?

The next verse, Romans 12:20, is God's directive for how we should respond to a hurtful offense. "If your enemy is hungry, feed him. If he is thirsty, give him a drink, for in so doing you will heap burning coals upon his head." For many years, I didn't understand what "heaping burning coals" on someone's head actually means. After all, it doesn't seem like a very kind thing to do to someone.

Then several years ago, Dr. Jay Adam's explanation of this verse enlightened me as to its true meaning. An expert in the Greek language, Dr. Adams explains that heaping burning coals was a very common and well-known military maneuver. When an army feared that their enemies were overtaking them and they could not escape, they would set the land behind them on fire. They ignited the fires to hold the enemy at bay. No army has ever successfully marched through fire.

When we respond properly to offenses, God will halt the pursuit of evil.

The fires effectively stopped the enemy's pursuit. The army could then escape or refortify themselves with necessary supplies. Godwants to do the same thing for us when our enemies pursue us. He wants to use the truths of His Word to stop the pursuit of evil.

Our natural inclination is to hurt someone back when he hurts us, but that violates God's command.

What does it mean to love your enemies? Jesus taught us in "The Sermon on the Mount" to love our enemies and to pray for them. This kind of love is not a sentimental affection. It's an agape love.

It is a 1 Corinthians 13 kind of love. Someone who loves with this kind of love is patient and kind. He is not jealous, rude, or easily provoked. People who love with agape love don't keep a score of offenses.

In Romans 12:21, the Apostle Paul summarizes God's strategy for dealing with conflict: "Do not be overcome by evil, but overcome evil with good." We usually feel a compelling urge to "pay someone back" when he or she offends us. Our natural inclination, however, is contrary to God's command to return good for evil. Christians who obey this command possess a powerful tool for reconciling and healing broken relationships.

They were so angry at each other I thought I might have to "break them up."

Two attorneys came to my office one day for counseling. I have seldom seen two people more at odds with one another than they were. What complicated matters even more was the fact that they were married to each other. Their anger was so intense during the first counseling session that at one point I thought I might have to step in between them. They seemed to hate each other.

I often give homework assignments at the end of a counseling appointment. I told them I had designed a project especially for them. I said I wanted them to treat each other like enemies for the next week. They exchanged utterly puzzled glances and the husband replied, "We seem to be doing a pretty good job of that already." "That's not what I'm talking about," I told them. Then I asked, "What does the Bible teach us about how to treat our enemies?" The husband taught a Sunday school class, and the wife was very involved in the women's ministry of their church. They understood, at that point, just what I meant them to do.

Jesus does not give us permission to treat our enemies cruelly. We must love them.

We love our enemies with agape love out of obedience to Jesus Christ. This is the kind of love I prescribed for this couple. I told them to be kind to one another and to return good deeds for any offenses they sustained. I explained hat we don't treat our enemies lovingly because they deserve it.

☐

They weren't supposed to analyze each other or analyze their marriage for one entire week.

I told them that for a period of one week, they weren't allowed to correct or criticize one another, or give each other unsolicited advice. I instructed them to avoid talking about their marriage relationship and how to fix it.

They were obviously unable to fix themselves at that point in time. The intensity of their conflict was so great that I feared for their children. Before they left my office, they shook hands and agreed to my requests. They made a commitment to me and to each other that for the next seven days, by God's grace, they would treat one another as enemies—with kindness and consideration.

Chapter 12

Offenders Reap What They Sow

One of the reasons why we naturally want to react against an offender is because our sense of justice has been violated. We must realize that God has a plan for carrying out justice and He needs no help from us. We can take consolation in the knowledge that God's holiness demands that all sins be addressed and dealt with. When we acknowledge and believe this truth, we can control our desire to retaliate against our offenders.

The sparring attorneys had made a commitment to refrain from all arguing and complaining for a period of seven days. Their homework assignment was to "treat each other like enemies." As they left my office at the conclusion of our first counseling session, I told them, "Be so nice to your spouse this week they'll think they died and went to heaven."

I hardly recognized the quarreling couple when they returned for their second appointment.

They were holding hands when they returned to my office the following week. They sat down together on a small loveseat next to my desk, and proceeded to snuggle up to each other. The affection they had begun to feel for one another was obvious. I could hardly believe these where the same people who had almost come to blows in my office a week earlier. They had chosen to obey God's command to return good for evil. In time, God rewarded their obedience with the blessing of a radically transformed relationship.

This couple, of course, obeyed more than this one principle alone. I met with them for approximately three months. I believe, however, that their willingness to obey God's Word that first week gave them a renewed motivation to put God first in their marriage relationship.

No one can escape the consequences of his choices in life.

Along with God's promise in Romans 12 to repay evildoers, we must consider Galatians 6:7: "Do not be deceived. God is not

□

mocked. Whatever a man sows, he will reap." This leads us to the next forgiveness principle.

Forgiveness Principle #4: An unrepentant offender has already begun to receive the consequences of his offense. This is a universal, non-optional principle of life.

When our sense of justice is violated we often tell ourselves, "That person shouldn't be allowed to get away with the deed he committed." But we find consolation in the knowledge that God's holiness demands that every single sin be dealt with according to His Word. He requires even His repentant children to bear the consequences of their choices.

We may think our enemies have gotten away with evil, but God vigilantly exercises His justice. When we acknowledge and believe this truth, we can more effectively resist the temptation to retaliate against our offenders.

We find these reassuring words in 2 Thessalonians 1:6: "After all, it is only just for God to repay with affliction, those who afflict you." We needlessly get ourselves into trouble when we try to help God repay this affliction. He doesn't need our help, and He doesn't want to hear our opinions on how or whom He should repay. He especially doesn't welcome our prayers in the matter.

In fact, we should never pray that God would execute judgment on our offenders. We read this warning in Proverbs 24: "Do not gloat when your enemy falls. When he stumbles, do not let your heart rejoice or the Lord will see and turn His wrath away from him."

The writer of Proverbs 11:21 declares: "Assuredly the evil man will not go unpunished. But the descendants of the righteous will be delivered." When we see an evildoer who appears to have gotten away with his sin, we should simply trust God and have faith that He will do what He promised to do.

We're responsible for obeying God's command to overcome evil with good.

When Christians refuse to forgive their offenders, or if they wish evil on them, they themselves will experience eternal consequences for their disobedience to the Lord. We must trust in God to punish evil and protect the righteous.

□

Adversity pursues an unrepentant sinner as relentlessly as hunting dogs pursue a raccoon.

Nighttime raccoon hunting is a Southern sport. The hunter sets his dogs loose and they chase the raccoon until it is treed. The chase is usually quite brief unless the raccoon happens to be particularly crafty. But the dogs are vigilant in their pursuit even after they become exhausted. They diligently stay on the raccoon's trail until they trap the animal so the hunter can come and kill it.

People may take advantage of your commitment to "return good for evil."

Someone who chooses to obey the command of Romans 12:21 to "overcome evil with good," risks the possibility that people may take advantage of his obedience. For example, many husbands have been known to take advantage of wives who've made this commitment to the Lord. However, the writer of Proverbs 17:13 warns: "He who returns evil for good, evil will not depart from his house."

Wives often express to me their fear that evil will befall their family because of a husband's disobedient lifestyle. I then explain to them a reassuring principle from God's Word. When God dispenses discipline and judgment upon the ungodly, His protective mercy preserves the righteous. We find an example of this in King Saul's life.

God did not hold Jonathan responsible for his father's sins.

God initially blessed King Saul abundantly. Then Saul drifted away from God. He began to grow increasingly jealous of David's success. God's judgment eventually fell upon Saul. He turned Saul over to his own mind, and dementia began to set in. Nevertheless, God blessed Saul's son Jonathan, and Jonathan's son Mephibosheth, because they had remained faithful to God. We must pray for God to be merciful and compassionate to our offenders.

When we witness God's judgment falling on an evildoer, we should pray for God's mercy on his/her life. We should be keenly aware of the fact that if any of us were to get what we deserve, we would receive eternal damnation. We should consistently pray for God to bestow compassion upon those people who have offended us and who have not sought our forgiveness.

Certain offenses that occur in the lives of Christians qualify as particularly traumatic.

I have counseled people who've been victims of such crimes as sexual molestation, aggravated assault and battery, rape, and attempted murder. This next principle of forgiveness, principle five, is the most powerful truth I've ever found, to lead such a counselee to the point of being willing to forgive his offender. This brings us to the fifth principle of forgiveness.

Forgiveness Principle #5: An offended person will experience eternal consequences in his life when he chooses to maintain an unforgiving response to an offense.

Peter approached Jesus in Matthew 18 and asked him, "Lord, how often shall my brother sin against me and I forgive him? Up to seven times?" Peter had a valid reason for using the number seven. The scribes taught that a person had to forgive an offender up to three times if he committed the offenses within a certain period of time.

Peter had already heard "The Sermon on the Mount," so he knew that Jesus had said, "Your righteousness must exceed that of the Scribes and the Pharisees." Peter, therefore, suggested a number that more than doubled the forgiveness quota the Scribes commonly taught people.

Jesus responded by telling Peter, in a manner of speaking, to put his mental ledger book away. He explained that God requires us to forgive our offenders an unlimited number of times.

Chapter 13

Forgiving Our Debtors

How can we who have been forgiven by Christ refuse to grant forgiveness to anyone for anything?

In Matthew 18, when Peter asks Jesus how often he is required to forgive a brother who sins against him. Jesus answers him with a phrase that was commonly used in that day, "seventy times seven." The phrase implied infinity. Through the story of a master and two hired servants, we learn why we are obligated to forgive our offenders each time they offend us.

Seven is a significant number in the Bible. Creation took place in seven days. The number seven appears 31 times in the Book of Revelation, alone. There are seven churches, seven vials and seven lamp stands, for example. It is a number that represents completeness or perfection.

Jesus told Peter we must forgive someone an infinite number of times.

Peter likely believed his suggestion of seven times was a generous one. But Jesus was telling Peter that there is no end to the number of times we are required to forgive our offenders.

The master had complete control over every aspect of the servant's life.

Then Jesus told a remarkable story of a master and two hired servants. One of the servants owed his master a large sum of money. The amount has been calculated to be the equivalent of $10 million dollars in silver. When the time arrived for the servant to repay the debt, he didn't have the money to pay his master. Therefore, in accordance with the laws of that day, the master ordered that all the servant's possessions be sold. He also ordered that the servant's wife and children be sold as slaves and that the servant be sold as a bond-slave.

When the servant cried out for mercy his master forgave him his debt.

This servant stood in danger of losing everything—his family, all of his rights, and his possessions. Scripture tells us he fell to his knees and begged his master for mercy. Seeing how pitiful and wretched the man was, the master was moved with compassion to forgive him his entire debt. Unfortunately, the story doesn't end there.

The servant who had been forgiven this enormous debt went out and found a fellow servant who owed him a small sum of money. He demanded that the fellow servant repay the debt, but he didn't have any money either. The fellow servant appealed for mercy just as the forgiven servant had previously appealed to his wealthy master. He begged, "Please be patient and I will pay you back all that I owe." But the forgiven servant was unwilling to forgive, and he had his fellow servant thrown into jail.

The ungrateful servant went out immediately and treated his fellow servant cruelly.

The forgiven servant, who had much to be thankful for, was angry, vengeful, and unmerciful. He continued to demand that his money be paid immediately. The debt of his fellow servant would not be considered an insignificant amount. It was the equivalent of approximately three months' salary for common labor of that day. However, compared to the debt that the first servant had been released from, it was a very small debt—what we might call a drop in the bucket.

News of the encounter between the two servants eventually reached the master's ears. He called for his servant to be brought to him. Then the master expressed his outrage and disbelief at what the wicked, ungrateful servant had done after having been forgiven so large a debt. We read in Matthew 18:34,35, "In anger his master turned him over to the jailers to be tortured until he should pay back all he owed." The master rescinded the cancellation of the $10 million-dollar debt.

Although many Christians miss the point of this story, it is one of the most instructive passages on the topic of forgiveness in all of Scripture. How can we who have been forgiven by Christ for all our sins refuse to grant forgiveness to anyone for anything?

When someone offends us and we feel we cannot forgive him, we should try to view that offense in light of the cross of Jesus Christ. As we recall how our sins nailed our Savior to the cross, our offender's sin against us begins to pale in comparison to our own transgressions against Holy God. We soon realize that if we refuse to forgive this individual, we are not worthy of the forgiveness that God has granted us in Jesus Christ.

The greatest offenses we sustain are small in comparison to our guilt before God.

We stand before God with an immeasurable debt of sin. Although people may commit large offenses against us, their offenses are small in comparison to our guilt before God. As Christians, we must acknowledge the magnitude of our own debt, and forgive those who offend us in the same way that God forgives us. This next case study of a young man who is falsely imprisoned, illustrates this principle of forgiveness.

We completely miss the lesson of the master and the wicked servant if we don't grasp the meaning of the final verse of Matthew 18. The master was angry with his unforgiving servant, and "he turned him over to the torturers until he should repay all that was owed him." In verse 35 Jesus sternly warns, "So shall my heavenly Father also do to you, if each of you does not forgive his brother from your heart."

We owe God a debt we could never repay.

This passage likens the great weight of our sin to the debt valued at $10 million dollars that the servant owed his master. We stand before God with an immeasurable debt of sin. Although many people may have committed significantly large offenses against us, their offenses are small in comparison to our guilt before God. The reverent fear of God, our Master, is a powerful incentive for us to obey the biblical principles of forgiveness.

Matt had been falsely accused and wrongly imprisoned.

This next case study is about a young man whose life was radically changed when he fully embraced the forgiveness principle demonstrated in the story of the master and the wicked servant. "Matt" was 21 years old when I met him. He came to my office with his pastor and proceeded to tell me what had happened to him. He had grown up in a Christian home in a rural community.

The family members who lived next door to him were not Christians. The father was a loud, angry man who got drunk almost every night. The son, "Jeremy," was Matt's best friend from the time they were about eight years old. They hunted, fished, and rode their four-wheelers together.

The Bible tells us, "Bad company corrupts good morals."

By the time Matt was 12 years old, Jeremy had introduced him to beer drinking. Apart from drinking beer, Matt had never done anything else to disobey his parents.

Matt took his car to the party because he never drank as much as his friends did.

Matt and Jeremy decided to attend a party one night when they were 18 years old, and they took Matt's car. He was usually more sober than anyone else at the end of the evening because he drank only enough to be accepted by his friends. He never really developed a taste for alcohol.

But Jeremy was at the wheel as they were driving home after the party that evening. Halfway home and very intoxicated, Jeremy swerved into the path of an oncoming car. The driver of the other car, a father of five children, was killed. All his children were in the car with him, and three of them were thrown from the car. All five children sustained serious injuries. Matt was also severely injured, but Jeremy had not been hurt at all. When the paramedics arrived at the scene of the accident, they found Jeremy there with Matt. Jeremy was the only person who was conscious. As he stood there in the dark and began to think through all that had transpired, he devised a story to protect himself from a possible prison sentence.

Jeremy faithfully stayed with Matt and applied pressure to his wounds.

When the paramedics examined Matt, they told Jeremy they did not think Matt would survive. They told him Matt had lost so much blood they were doubtful he'd even make it to the hospital. They instructed Jeremy to stay with Matt and apply pressure to his wounds, which were bleeding profusely. Then they left to care for the injured children. Jeremy did as he was told and stayed with Matt until the back-up ambulance unit arrived.

Matt never saw Jeremy the entire time he was in the hospital.

Matt did not die, but he was in a coma for the next six weeks. Both his legs and arms were broken, and his jaw was wired together. He stayed in the hospital for several months, and during that time Jeremy never came to see him once. Jeremy told his friends that seeing Matt in that condition would bring back too many horrible memories of the night the wreck occurred.

No one believed Matt would be sentenced to a prison term.

Matt's trial date arrived several months later. His attorneys had assured him he would not have to go to jail. This was his first driving offense. He had never even gotten a speeding ticket, and he was genuinely sorry for what he had done. Matt had been horrified to learn he had killed someone, and he agonized over the children's injuries. He had written letters of apology to all the family members.

Matt's attorney told him he would probably lose his driver's license and be ordered to attend an alcohol treatment program. The attorney predicted that the judge would probably place Matt on probation for three years. The attorney could not have foreseen the influence that Mothers Against Drunk Drivers would have on the outcome of this trial. The group began to work on behalf of the three children who still had substantial injuries one year after the accident. They publicized the trial and pressured the state attorney not to make any deals. At his trial, Matt was sentenced to 15 years in the state penitentiary.

One of Matt's friends found out what had really happened the night of the accident.

On the day of Matt's sentencing, another one of his friends went to the police with a shocking story. He had gone to visit Jeremy the day after the accident. He was going to knock on the door when he heard someone inside yelling loudly. He stood there for a few moments, afraid to proceed, and then he heard the father shout, "How could you do this again? You've already gotten two DUI's (Driving Under the Influence), and now because of your drinking and driving you've threatened your best friend's life! Will you ever learn your lesson?" As the friend stood there outside the door that afternoon, he realized that Jeremy was the one who was driving the night the wreck occurred.

It would be impossible to get Matt released from prison unless more evidence was found.

When Matt was sentenced to prison, the friend finally decided to tell Matt's parents what he had heard a year earlier. He didn't want to live with the guilt of knowing that an innocent man was in prison. Matt's parents were shocked by the information and went directly to the state attorney. He told them Matt's conviction could not be overturned based upon hearsay evidence. However, he agreed to conduct a more thorough investigation of the accident vehicle. They hadn't investigated the car previously because Jeremy had been an eyewitness.

The investigator who went back to the car discovered that some hair was embedded in the shattered windshield on the *passenger's* side. It was an established fact that Matt's head had hit the windshield before he was thrown from the car, so they phoned the prison to request a sample of Matt's hair. Then they sent both samples to the new DNA lab that had recently opened in Washington, DC. Their discovery? The two hair samples matched!

Matt couldn't wait to get out of prison so he could kill Jeremy and then kill himself.

A United States congressman began the process of getting Matt released from prison. He had been there for 15 months and had been severely beaten up and repeatedly sodomized by older fellow-prisoners. He told me the only thing that kept him going during those months in prison was the thought that when he got out of prison he would kill Jeremy and then kill himself. His parents and his pastor picked him up from prison the day he was released, and two days later he was sitting in my office. He flatly refused to even consider forgiving Jeremy until I explained that he would experience eternal consequences unless he changed his mind.

Matt finally agreed to forgive his former friend who had sent him to prison.

For several days, Matt couldn't eat or sleep. The fear of God was powerfully motivating him to reconsider. When he returned to my office he announced that he was ready to forgive Jeremy, although he had no feelings of forgiveness for him. He chose to forgive Jeremy out of his will, and the dramatic transformation that took place in Matt's life, thereafter, was nothing short of miraculous.

Chapter 14

Becoming Like My Offender

If our goal is *not* to be like someone, we often become like him because our focus is not on Jesus.

Forgiveness Principle #6: When we withhold forgiveness from someone, we run the risk of becoming just like him, in attitudes, if not in actions.

In this chapter, we explore how a pattern of reactionary responses occurs between husbands and wives who are experiencing marital conflict. It can begin to happen shortly after marriage, and may continue to go on for years before the couple seeks objective, biblical help.

Spouses often relate to their partners in the same way their parents related to one another. This happens in spite of the fact that they are determined not to repeat their parents' mistakes. The problem is that their focus is on *not* becoming like a particular individual, rather than on becoming more like Jesus Christ.

Every week in my counseling practice, I see marriages that are in trouble. Over the years, I've observed a pattern of reactionary responses that occurs between husbands and wives. They usually begin the pattern by harshly criticizing one another. Within a short period of time, they progress to the next stage, where the husband generally commits some sort of selfish or insensitive act. Then the wife reacts to him with an unloving attitude.

The husband excuses his wrong actions by telling himself that his wife's attitude is a far worse offense.

Next, the husband decides that his wife's wrong attitude is worse than his initial offense and soon a reaction sequence is established between them. This can occur within a few months, or even weeks after two people get married. Husbands and wives are sometimes caught up in the reaction sequence deadlock for the span of their entire marriage. When one or both partners begin to focus on the wrong things in their relationship, they establish this reaction sequence pattern.

Our focus should be on imitating the Lord Jesus Christ.

Many newlyweds determine, "I won't be the kind of husband my father was," or "I'll make sure that I won't be the kind of parent my mother was." The problem with this kind of thinking is that when our goal is to be *unlike* someone, we focus our attention directly on that person—and not on Jesus Christ.

However, God wants us to focus so intently on being like the Lord Jesus that His character pervades every aspect of our lives. We should be thinking about Him and comparing ourselves to Him. In Romans 2:1,2 Paul admonishes us: "You, therefore, have no excuse, you who pass judgment on someone else. For whatever point you judge the other, you are condemning yourself because…you do the same things."

One day a physician I worked with interrupted one of my counseling sessions. He asked me to go to his examining room and talk with "Jim," one of his patients whom he feared was having an emotional breakdown. Jim was weeping so hard I could hardly understand what he was saying. I finally got the full story.

This husband appeared to be having a complete breakdown in his doctor's office.

Both he and his wife were committed Christians who were active members of their church. They had been married for several years. He had no idea his marriage was in trouble until his wife asked him to leave. Jim pleaded with me, "Can you please get my wife in here so she can explain to you what the problem is? She says she can't tell me."

So I met with his wife and she told me, "The main problem is that he's just like his father." Jim's father was an alcoholic who owned a liquor store. When he wasn't drinking, he was a nice, friendly man who would do anything to help someone in need. But one or two drinks of alcohol drastically altered his personality. He would become angry and aggressive, often abusing his wife and children. I knew this woman was not married to an abusive drunkard. Jim was a committed Christian who'd never had a drink of alcohol in his life. Yet, when I considered Forgiveness Principle #6, I understood exactly what the problem was.

□

Jim would help his brothers and sisters escape through a window so his father wouldn't hurt them.

When Jim was a child his father would frequently come home in a drunken rage. Jim would often have to help his three younger siblings climb out of a window and run to a neighbor's house, so his father wouldn't hurt them. He never knew what his mother would look like the next morning when they came home after their father had left for work. She sometimes had black eyes and bruises on her face and arms. On one occasion she had a broken nose and a chipped tooth.

His mother was a Christian who diligently tried to raise her four children in the nurture of the Lord. In spite of their hostile living environment, she succeeded. When Jim was sixteen years old, he committed his life to Jesus Christ. Soon he discovered his father was having a series of affairs with various women. He would say to himself every day, "When I'm grown, I'll never be like that man."

In his early twenties, Jim married a Christian girl and they pledged to each other that their home would be Christ-centered. They had three children and things seemed to go very well for several years. Then his wife asked him to move out. I knew that besides not drinking alcoholic beverages, Jim didn't beat his wife or children, and he had never committed adultery. Yet, his wife persisted in her accusation that he was exactly like his father. She explained that he was often harsh and angry, just as his father had been during his drunken rages.

Her parents believed she should divorce her husband because of his anger.

Her parents were making the situation worse by encouraging her to get a divorce. They told her, "Men can't really change. He'll change just enough to get back into the house and then he'll go right back to his old ways." They didn't want their daughter to continue living in an unhappy marriage, and they didn't want her to raise their grandchildren in an angry, hostile environment.

When I reported to Jim, I explained that his wife believed he was exactly like his father. I told him he would be unable to change until he fully forgave his father. His reaction was dramatic. "I love my father," he protested loudly. "He hasn't had a drink in ten years and he treats my mother better than he ever did before." He continued, "We go fishing together, we have a peach stand together, and we're closer than we've ever been. He has changed and I don't have any animosity or resentment toward him." "I have completely forgiven my father," he concluded. Yet, I knew for certain, he had not forgiven him.

Jim and I began to work through the principles of biblical forgiveness. It soon became obvious that he had never taken the necessary steps to forgive his father for all the offenses he had committed against him, his siblings, and his mother when he was growing up.

Jim eagerly completed his homework assignments and he demonstrated a humble, teachable spirit.

I can usually tell if a counselee is grasping the various principles as we go through them. Jim was giving himself completely to the process. He diligently completed all the projects I gave him each Week and he came to understand the biblical principles of forgiveness over the course of the next several weeks. At the end of the counseling process he forgave his father for the first time in his life.

His father-in-law offered to pay for the divorce.

Jim's wife's parents continued to urge their daughter to get a divorce. They even offered to pay for it. I was pleading with her, on the other hand, to give Jim one more chance. I assured her that I felt certain we had dealt with the root issues in his life. I asked her to give him the opportunity to prove to her that there had been a change in his character and in his attitude.

Jim's wife finally agreed to a trial period of reconciliation.

After they had been separated for five months she agreed to a 30-day trial reconciliation. We promised her that, if at the end of one month she still didn't care for Jim's behavior, all she had to do was express her dissatisfaction to me. He would then leave voluntarily, grant her a divorce and continue to financially support her and the children. Realizing she had nothing to lose and everything to gain, she agreed to the arrangement.

Jim moved back home and the month went remarkably well. He had resolved his root problems. Each day Jim experienced unprecedented grace to overcome his life-dominating struggle with harshness and anger. His gentleness and patience amazed his wife.

She expected to witness outbursts of anger but he consistently demonstrated self-control. His willingness to take responsibility for his actions and his attitudes established the foundation for them to begin living together joyfully and harmoniously.

I heard from Jim one year later. He reported that he and his wife were doing better than they'd ever done.

Jim phoned me one year later on the anniversary of the date he had moved back home. He told me his wife had recently expressed that she was happier than she'd ever been in her life. She told him she could never have envisioned the changes that had taken place in his character and in his attitudes. Jim concluded, "We want you to know that we praise God for what He has done in our marriage."

The biblical principles of forgiveness can bring about powerful changes in any relationship, no matter how damaged or broken it may be. We must realize, as Jim did, that when we fail to forgive an offender, we risk becoming like him in attitudes, if not in actions.

Chapter 15

Growing in the Midst of Trials

Christians experience the most significant spiritual growth in the midst of trials and suffering.

Have you ever wondered why bad things happen to good people? Because of our sin nature, none of us welcome trials into our lives. We learn to embrace hardships, however, as we grow in Christ, and as we begin to experience the benefits that result from suffering. Believers can't derive the fullest benefit from their problems until they understand why God allows them to occur. Christians must yield their hearts and minds to the process of learning a biblical view of suffering.

Of all the principles of biblical forgiveness that appear in Scripture, the one we'll discuss now is particularly profound: God commands His children to embrace the trials in their lives.

God doesn't send us trials and suffering to punish us for our disobedience.

False teachings abound suggesting that we experience suffering because of disobedience to God. Yet the opposite is actually true. God wants us to discern the benefits, insights, and opportunities that result from suffering. As we progress in our spiritual journey over time, we gradually learn to accept our problems and hardships as a normal part of the Christian life.

We have a natural aversion to pain and suffering, but it is "in the flames" that we grow the most.

Some Christians mistakenly believe that the only means of spiritual growth are prayer, Bible-reading, church attendance, and ministry involvement. All of these disciplines are of supreme importance and we shouldn't minimize them. However, it's an undeniable fact we experience the most significant spiritual growth in the midst of our problems and trials.

The writer of 1 Peter 4:12 exhorts us: "Beloved, do not be

surprised at the fiery ordeal among you, which comes upon you for your testing, as though some strange thing were happening to you." God is in our trials and He has a purpose for every offense, irritation, and hurt we have ever endured.

Forgiveness Principle #7: We cannot welcome our trials or derive the fullest benefit from our problems until we understand why God allows them to occur.

Over the years of my counseling practice, many former counselees have returned to express their gratitude for having learned how to practically implement this principle in their lives.

Christians and non-Christians alike, commonly ask the question, "Why do bad things happen to good people, and why is there so much pain and suffering in this world?" I've had a special interest in this subject for years. Thus, I've read every book and magazine article I can find on this topic, many of which are excellent treatments of this perplexing question. Elisabeth Elliot, John MacArthur, Charles Stanley, and Kay Arthur have all written outstanding books addressing this subject from a biblical perspective. Almost every writer who contributes significantly to the evangelical scene has written a book on this topic. It's a pertinent question that everyone must deal with.

What do we say to the parents of a four year-old girl who was run over and killed? How do we offer substantive help and hope to a wife whose ex-husband brutally beat her and left her for dead? How can we biblically encourage a ten year-old girl who had to crawl over her brother's body to get out of a car demolished by a drunk driver?

In my counseling practice, I deal with these kinds of situations for hours each week. Most Christians don't know how to discern God's purposes for suffering. If we want to learn how to forgive biblically, however, we must yield our hearts and minds to the necessary process of learning to embrace our trials.

Many Christians mistakenly believe God should grant them immunity from trials and suffering.

When tragic situations occur, Believers often want to know if they can ever trust God again. Counselees frequently ask me, "Why do Christians have to endure pain and suffering?" They love God and they're certain God loves them. So they conclude that He should grant them some degree of immunity from major hardships in their lives. Every follower of Christ needs to learn to evaluate how God uses our trials to accomplish specific purposes in our lives.

The young boy did not realize that his little sister was not following him this time.

Let's consider two counseling situations that vividly illustrate the need to answer this question regarding pain and suffering. The first illustration is about a four year-old girl. One week-day afternoon she and her eight-year old brother were playing indoors when they heard the loud speaker of an ice-cream truck blaring outside their home.

They were thrilled when their mother gave them money. She told the boy to hold his little sister's hand on the way to the truck. Excited about the cold treat they were about to enjoy, he carefully

led her to the ice-cream truck and bought their cones. After paying the vendor, he turned to go back inside, thinking his sister was following along behind him, as she had done many times before.

The driver of the truck pulled forward and unknowingly ran over the little girl.

The driver slid back into his seat, started the engine and began to pull forward. He didn't know the little girl had walked around the truck and sat down on the front right bumper to eat her ice-cream cone. And he didn't see her when she fell off the bumper onto the road. The truck crushed her to death as the driver pulled forward. Two weeks after the accident occurred, some friends of the family brought this child's parents to my office. They were angry at the man who killed their daughter, and they were angry at their son. Most of all, they were angry at God. They wanted to know why a loving God would allow this tragedy to happen.

After beating her nearly to death, her ex-husband planned to burn her alive.

The second illustration is the story of a woman whose ex-husband broke into her home, brutally raped her, and savagely beat her into unconsciousness with a handgun. He then doused the house with gasoline and set it on fire. As she smelled the gasoline fumes, she momentarily regained consciousness. She stumbled out the front door where neighbors saw her as she collapsed. They called an ambulance and the police. The doctors were amazed she survived after having lost so much blood. Weeks later, when she came to my office for counseling, she wanted some answers. How could God love her if He let her go through such a horrible ordeal? Could she ever trust Him again?

Some of us may have experienced similar tragedies in our lives. On the other hand, we may be facing a trial that, though it may not be as dramatic as the two illustrations we've considered, is nonetheless defeating us spiritually and robbing us of our joy in the Lord.

Some people may be experiencing problems in their marriage relationships. Perhaps they're staying together for the sake of their children. There may be parents who have a rebellious teenager who seems to be rejecting all of the values and truths that they deem important. There may be teens who believe they have unreasonable parents and they feel unable to communicate with them. Other people may be dealing with conflicts at church or at their workplace.

As we identify the trials we're facing we can begin to determine what benefits God has for us in our present suffering.

Identify and write down whatever difficulties you are presently facing in your life. Then use the questions at the end of this chapter to evaluate how God may be using these trials to accomplish certain things in your life that probably wouldn't be accomplished through any other means. Begin the process of discerning God's benefits in the midst of your trials.

God uses our problems and difficulties as a means to develop His character within us.

We sometimes forget how dependent we are upon God. When painful circumstances occur in our lives, we should remember that God has not forgotten us. He often uses the difficulty of a particular situation to remind us of our weakness, and of our critical need for Him and for other people. God wants to teach us that apart from His mercy, we are helpless, and utterly in need of His grace.

I often explain to counselees that God uses the problems we encounter and the difficulties we face as a means to develop His character within us. The following questions and accompanying scripture verses are helpful for anyone who wants to learn more about why God allows His children to undergo trials and suffering.

"Evaluating God's Character Development"

As you read the questions, rate each of your answers on a scale from **1-10.** If you read a particular question that doesn't seem to apply to your situation, mark it "1." If you're certain the question clearly applies to you, mark it "10." The 1-10 scale is a suggested tool to give you some idea of how much each statement applies to your situation. This is not an objective test. It is meant to encourage those who take it, and no one can fail it.

Question #1 – Is the difficulty of this circumstance a reminder of my weakness, and of my critical need for God and for other people? _____

A "critical need for God" means you're completely helpless apart from His mercy, and you're wholly dependent upon His grace. It means God is essential and foundational to every aspect of your life. Is God using the pain associated with this situation to show you that you need your Heavenly Father first and foremost?

Is He demonstrating to you how much you need the support of other people? God didn't design the Christian life to be lived independently. We're *interdependent* creatures who need accountability and encouragement.

Paul actually delighted in his weaknesses because God proved Himself strong on his behalf.

Paul states in 2 Corinthians 12:9-10, "My grace is sufficient for you, for My power is made perfect in weakness. Therefore I will boast all the more gladly about my weaknesses, so that Christ's power may rest on me. That is why, for Christ's sake, I delight in weaknesses, in insults, in hardships, in persecutions, in difficulties. For when I am weak, then I am strong."

Was Paul's "thorn in the flesh" his wife?

The apostle Paul had a problem he referred to as his "thorn in the flesh." Theologians love to debate the question of what that thorn may have been. Several popular theories exist. Some people contend the thorn referred to Paul's wife. He may actually have been married in his earlier years because he was a member of the Sanhedrin Council. One of the qualifications for membership in the Sanhedrin was that a man had to be married. We know, however, that he was single by the time he wrote 1 Corinthians because he tells us there that he was single.

Although many people died after receiving a scourging, Paul survived five brutal scourgings—and flourished.

Many people believe Paul's thorn in the flesh was some kind of physical infirmity. We find in the book of Acts that the citizens of Lystra stoned Paul, dragged him outside the city gate, and left him for dead. Paul endured the dangers of shipwrecks, scourgings, and the bite of a venomous snake.

All this misery and ill treatment, no doubt, exacted a heavy toll on Paul's body. Yet, based upon what the passage says, his "thorn" probably was not physical. It's likely that God designed Paul's "thorn in the flesh" to remind him of his weakness, and to keep him utterly dependent upon the Lord.

God refused to relieve Paul of his "thorn in the flesh."

When we come to God humbly, admitting our great need for Him, He delights in meeting our needs. Paul writes in 2 Corinthians 12:8, "Concerning this, I entreated the Lord three times that it might depart from me." He prayed fervently to be delivered of his problem. We would generally expect Paul's prayers to be answered. He saw the resurrected Christ and he performed miracles, as did the other apostles. Yet God responded to Paul's request with an emphatic "no."

In spite of every imaginable hardship, Paul never gave up.

God told Paul, "My grace is sufficient for you, for My power is made perfect through weakness." This weakness does not refer to some moral problem Paul was struggling with. The Greek word for this type of weakness means "a problem I cannot solve." Paul had a problem he could not solve himself. He tells us in 2 Corinthians 12 that he was content with weaknesses, insults, distresses, and hardships so Christ's power could rest on him. That is why Paul endured to the end, persevering through trials and persecution—for Christ's sake.

Do you have any problems in your life that you can't solve? Have people insulted you with harsh, angry words? Have people treated you unkindly and inconsiderately? Have you endured hardships and painful situations?

Christians experience a surprising amount of persecution in their families.

Have you been persecuted? Persecution is when people ridicule and abuse you for doing what's right. Christians often undergo significant persecution within their own families. Teenagers rebel against the loving provision and authority of their parents. Husbands and wives, who should love each other above everyone else, persecute their spouse for trying to live a righteous life. Persecution frequently occurs in the workplace where work associates act vindictively, or an employer shows partiality.

As I learn the backgrounds of some of my counselees and as I become acquainted with their particular trials, I often tell them this passage in 2 Corinthians 12 could be a commentary on their lives.

Some of us have faced situations when we needed the Lord so much we knew we wouldn't make it unless He supernaturally intervened in our lives. But most of us don't really believe Paul's declaration, "When I am weak, then I am strong."

In the midst of our weakness we learn how desperately we need the Lord. We begin to realize that if God doesn't break through our pain with provision and help, we may not make it. Anytime we come to God in a spirit of humility, admitting our great need for Him, He delights in meeting our needs.

Question #2 – Is God using this situation to call me to a self-examination of my life, in relation to God and to others? _____

The writer of 1 Corinthians 11:28 instructs us, "Let every man examine himself." This self-examination does not refer to the ongoing evaluations that Christians strive to do on a regular basis. God commands us to consistently consider our attitudes, scrutinize our motives, and maintain peaceful relationships with other people.

This question refers, instead, to an intensive, Psalm 139:23 type of self-examination: "Search me, O God, and know my heart; test me and know my anxious thoughts. See if there is any wicked way in me."

If God is using a difficult situation in your life to lead you in this direction, your trial will be relentless until you're willing to obey His call to intensively examine your heart before Him.

God often brings trials and difficult circumstances into our lives in order to deal with our pride. We teach children from an early age that pride is a virtue. Our self-worth is often wrapped up in how well we perform in certain areas of life, such as sports or music. We thrive on the affirmation we receive, and the admiration boosts our self-esteem. Let's turn our attention now to two major ways that pride usually manifests itself—loud obnoxiousness and stubborn independence. The words of Proverbs 11:2 challenge us, "When pride comes, then comes disgrace, but with humility comes wisdom."

I'm always a little hesitant when the time arrives in a counseling session to discuss this third evaluation question. Each time I teach this principle, vivid memories flood my mind and God reminds me anew why He allowed me to go through the trials I faced in the early years of my marriage.

Question #3 – Is God using this situation to deal with my pride? _____

My wife and I had been committed Christians for several years before we got married. Yet we both had an attitude of pride that made us unwilling to yield to God's transforming power in our lives.

As I was growing up pride was a desirable quality.

My parents raised me in an environment where people considered pride a virtue. I was involved in athletic pursuits for most of the first 19 years of my life. I played football, basketball, and baseball. All our coaches throughout those years sought to instill a strong sense of pride in us.

I remember the Friday night football games when the coach would gather the whole team in the locker room to give us the traditional pre-game pep talk. He would remind us of our twice-a-day practices in the relentless Florida August heat. He would commend us for the sacrifices we had made and the physical pain we had endured. Then he would shout with conviction, "Your parents are here tonight! Your girlfriends are here! The cheerleaders will be yelling for you and the band will be playing for you! We've got TV cameras and newspaper reporters ready to see what you can do!

Now get out there men, and show 'em what you're worth!"

Our self-worth was wrapped up in how well we played sports.

I recall the adrenaline pumping and the enthusiastic promises, "Yes Sir, Coach! We're gonna stomp 'em! We're gonna kill 'em!" Then we'd go out on the field and the other team would demolish us almost every time. But we didn't care, because we still got the

attention and admiration from our peers. We still got our names in the newspaper. All the pain was worth it. All the attention we received boosted our sagging self-esteem. Sadly enough, our self-worth was based on our athletic ability. Unfortunately, the praise we received for our minimal athletic prowess served to reinforce our pride.

I had never been accused of being proud until I got married.

The sin of pride manifests itself in two distinctly different ways. The obnoxious, self-promoting person is obviously proud. We easily recognize this individual, since he's often loud and inconsiderate. This type of individual is "outwardly" proud. But there are also people who are "inwardly" proud.

As I was growing up no one accused me of being proud. I had observed enough outwardly proud people that I had learned how to avoid appearing proud. I even knew how to appear humble and meek. My wife was the only person in my life that accused me of being proud. You can probably imagine how angry that made me. God knew I was an inwardly proud person. This kind of pride often manifests itself in stubbornness, and that's exactly how my wife perceived me. I was self-sufficient and I demonstrated an independent spirit. This is the kind of pride that destroys marriages. The writer of Proverbs 11:2 accurately predicted my outcome, "When pride comes then comes disgrace, but with humility comes wisdom."

Common grace is the restraining power of God that prevented us from being as wicked as we could have been before He saved us from our sin. However, God grants us a different kind of grace at the point of salvation—saving grace. When we gain a clear understanding of what God has contributed to our lives, we begin to revere God, and become less self-satisfied.

Humility is the recognition that any good, whatsoever, that we possess in our lives is the result of God's grace. *Common grace* is one particular manifestation of God's grace.

If common grace did not exist, mankind would soon destroy itself.

The *saving grace* of God is different from common grace. God grants us saving grace in Jesus Christ, and through it, He gives us a new heart, a new life, new motivations, and new desires. Romans 3:10-20 is God's description of the condition of the human heart. For many years I read this passage of Scripture impassively, unable to identify with the kind of person these verses describe: "As it is written, 'There is no one righteous, not even one. There is no one who understands, no one who seeks God. All have turned away; they have together become worthless. There is no one who does good, not even one.' "

Note the term "no one, not even *one*." Then it gets worse: "Their throats are open graves. Their tongues practice deceit. The poison of vipers is on their lips. Their mouths are full of cursing and bitterness. Their feet are swift to shed blood; ruin and misery mark their ways, and the way of peace they do not know. There is no fear of God before their eyes."

I often thought, "I'm sure glad I'm not as bad as that!"

Each time I read this passage in Romans 3 I would think, "I'm not convinced I was ever quite *that* bad." "After all," I reasoned, "I was a pretty good kid and I was a committed Christian from the time I was 16 years old. I never once rebelled against my parents." Yet, according to this passage, everyone fits this description.

I finally came to understand the truth of these vitally important verses. We would all be exactly like the person who is described here were it not for the common grace and the saving grace of God. This passage would characterize everyone, apart from God's grace, in a very short amount of time.

Are we involved in petty quarrels and selfish disagreements?

We learn more about the sin of pride in Proverbs 13:10: "Pride breeds quarrels, conflicts, disagreements, and controversies." God reassures us in James 4:6, "He opposes the proud but He gives grace to the humble. Submit yourself then to God." Pride is one of our greatest hindrances as we seek to live a successful Christian life.

God faithfully disciplines His children for the sin of pride. He unfailingly purges pride from our lives. One of the main ways He accomplishes this is by allowing us to go through circumstances that humble us. He shows us a picture of ourselves in relation to His holiness. He gives us a clearer understanding of what He has contributed to our lives. The more we know and revere God, the less satisfied we become with ourselves.

Jesus begins the Sermon on the Mount with the words, "Blessed are the poor in spirit." In the midst of suffering God teaches us to be poor in spirit. The path through trials is difficult, humbling, and even humiliating at times, but it is the pathway to blessings and grace. Jesus intentionally began the Beatitudes in the Sermon on the Mount with the words, "Blessed are the poor in spirit."

People who are poor in spirit realize that they are nothing apart from God's grace.

The great theologian David Martin Lloyd-Jones defines poverty of spirit as "the recognition, as we stand before God, that we are nothing, we have nothing, we can do nothing, and we stand in need of all things."

At first, I couldn't figure out why most church workers seemed to be proud.

Over the course of the last 20 years, I've counseled many pastors, church staff members, missionaries, and para-church workers. Most of these counselees share a common problem. They often demonstrate a very proud spirit. This puzzled me, at first. I reasoned that these ministers of God's Word should be especially humble and meek. After all, they're paid to spend extra time studying God's Word and praying. Yet, I kept encountering this persistent problem of pride.

We tell ministerial students that their knowledge qualifies them to minister.

After spending some time analyzing the situation, I concluded that the root of the problem lies in how we train pastors for the ministry. We send men off to Seminary and we remove them from the mainstream of life.

We cram their brains full of Greek and Hebrew, systematic theology, church history, evangelism, and missions, hour after hour, day after day, for three years or more. They accumulate a massive amount of information and knowledge. We give them a diploma and tell them they are now qualified to minister. Scripture warns us, however, "Knowledge puffs up."

We fail to adequately prepare Seminary graduates before we send them out to minister.

We unwittingly inflate their egos by telling them in so many words, "You *are* what you *know*." Then we send them out with very little experience, humility, or wisdom, to confuse and frustrate the first two or three congregations that hire them. That is *not* how Jesus trained his disciples.

Some Seminary programs today are changing the way they approach theological education. We should commend them for their effort to move away from the traditional methods that seem to reinforce pride in ministerial students. They are finding innovative ways to train ministers in a more biblical manner.

I must be diligent to repent of pride in my own life. Pride is a sin that threatens to quickly undo us.

God reminds me of the need to carefully examine my own heart each time I identify a proud spirit in a counselee. As we encounter trials and hardships, we must ask our heavenly Father to bring us once again to the point of poverty of spirit before Him.

Each time God gives us a glimpse of the pride in our heart, we can draw encouragement from the words of Proverbs 11:2: "When pride comes, then comes disgrace, but with humility comes wisdom." God leads us on a humbling path through our trials to grant us more of His godly wisdom. He teaches us in the midst of suffering, to be poor in spirit.

God often uses difficult circumstances to get our attention and keep it focused on Him.

If you want to know whether God is using the trials in your life to focus your attention on Him, you must determine your level of commitment to Him. God expects His children to obey Him promptly and willingly. He will lovingly and faithfully discipline any willfulness that exists in your heart. Your obedience pleases Him and He will not tolerate lukewarm, inconsistent commitment.

Scripture addresses our disobedience in Jeremiah 35:14: "I have spoken to you again and again, yet you have not obeyed Me." The Bible contains many verses related to the subject of sacrifice. We find, however, in 1 Samuel 15:22, that God values obedience more highly than sacrifice.

God does not tolerate disobedience in His children's lives.

As we continue to evaluate how God uses our trials to develop His character in our lives, we must understand that He lovingly disciplines any willfulness that exists in our heart.

Question #4 – Is God using this circumstance to get my attention and keep me focused on Him? _____

I've found that God seldom has to *get* the attention of most committed Christians. The second half of this question is more pertinent to our investigation. Is God working in my life to *keep* my attention *riveted* on Him?

"Hot" and "cold" Christians are easily discernible.

In the Book of Revelation, God identifies three kinds of people. The first kind is one who is *hot* in his relationship with the Lord. This individual is deeply committed to walk in obedience to Christ, and has a testimony of consistent faithfulness. When other people encounter this *hot* Christian, they tend to respond in one of two ways. Some find that his peaceful countenance and joyful enthusiasm encourage and inspire them. Others don't care to associate with this person, because when they spend time with him they feel God's conviction regarding their own lack of commitment.

The second kind of person is described as *cold* toward the Lord. These people may be agnostics, who don't really know what they believe, or atheists, who dramatically contend that God doesn't exist. Or they may even be adherents to other religions such as Buddhism, Islam, Hinduism, and the New Age Movement.

A "lukewarm" Christian *looks* a lot like a "hot" Christian.

The passage in Revelation refers to the third kind of person as *lukewarm* in his faith. These individuals profess to be Believers in the Lord Jesus Christ, but are generally inconsistent in their Christian walk. They are typically indifferent to certain scriptural responsibilities, and may struggle with life-dominating sin habits. They are often disobedient to the basic biblical commands a Believer must obey to successfully live the Christian life.

The interesting thing is that outwardly, *lukewarm* Christians appear to be very similar to *hot* Christians. If you looked around a typical church congregation on a Sunday morning, you wouldn't be able to readily determine who was lukewarm towards God and who was hot. These two types of Christians even talk alike. Lukewarm Christians generally have spent some part of their lives within an organized church and they know the language.

They go to church and they talk the talk. They may even put money in the offering plate. Yet, if we spent a substantial amount of time with them or if we lived with them, we'd quickly discern their level of commitment. If you want to know whether or not God is trying to get your attention, first, prayerfully discern which of these three categories you fall into.

Emotional defeat, discouragement and depression all typify a lukewarm Christian lifestyle.

Are you experiencing depression? Let's take a look now at the 3-"d's" of lukewarm Christianity. The first is spiritual and emotional *defeat* because a lukewarm Christian doesn't utilize God-given resources to walk victoriously. The second "d" is *discouragement* because he's unable to experience consistent spiritual growth and he quickly becomes discouraged in his walk with the Lord. The third "d" is *depression*.

Believers must seek to be wholeheartedly committed and obedient to the Lord.

He is aware that God's hand of discipline is upon his life and he no longer possesses the joy and peace that were formerly his. This inevitably leads to depression.

When God's hand of discipline is upon us, depression is sure to follow.

I recently did a study on the "hand" of God. Motivated by the fact that I've never heard a sermon or seen a book on this topic, I studied every Scripture passage referring to God's hand. I found several references to the heavy hand of God resting upon His disobedient children. Depression will eventually overcome someone who's living under God's hand of discipline. Today most psychologists and psychiatrists, even many Christian psychologists, have concluded that a chemical imbalance in the body causes depression. I don't discount the fact that certain physiological causes for depression exist. Frequently, however, when a doctor discovers that a patient's seratonin level is lower than it should be, he or she recommends antidepressant medication, without investigating other possibilities.

When we feel depressed, we shouldn't automatically conclude that an antidepressant drug is the remedy.

I don't doubt that most depressed people feel better when they take antidepressant drugs. Often, they feel happier or calmer. Sometimes they feel lethargic. Yet, for over 20 years I've dealt with people who take antidepressant medication, and I've observed that the use of these drugs often diminishes, among other things, their creative drive—that unique dynamic that enables them to accomplish great things for God. Christians who are experiencing depression should prayerfully rethink the assumption that antidepressant medication is the answer.

When we're depressed, we must attempt to deal with our problem from a biblical perspective. I've witnessed the emotional and spiritual deliverance of thousands of people who were willing to respond biblically to their battle with depression.

Determine which spiritual category you fall into—hot, cold, or lukewarm.

Many of us may never have experienced the emotionally crippling effects of depression. But it's vitally important, nonetheless, for us to decide whether or not we're living in a lukewarm spiritual state. Many counselees tell me they would describe their level of commitment to Jesus Christ as somewhere between lukewarm and hot. I tell them that there is no such biblical category.

God tells us in Revelation 3:15,16: "I know your deeds, that you are neither cold, nor hot. I would that you are cold or hot, so because you are lukewarm, and neither hot nor cold, I will spit you out of my mouth." This word "spit" is also translated from the Greek, as "vomit." Lukewarm Christians are so offensive to God that He won't allow them to continue in their half-hearted commitment to Him. He will vomit them out of His mouth. He wants our wholehearted love, our willing obedience and our full devotion. When we drift into a lukewarm state God often sends us a trial to jolt us to attention.

God sometimes brings trials into our lives to force us to cry out to Him for help and wisdom.

We may have problems with our health, our marriage, our job or our church. Whenever problems occur we usually try to solve them ourselves. Soon we find ourselves even more defeated and depressed. God wants to teach us to find solutions to our problems by seeking His help and wisdom. He wants us to fall on our face before Him and cry out for His grace and provision.

Are you settling for a lifestyle of lukewarm commitment to the Lord? Is He sending you a wake-up call in the form of some trial?

We can't help ourselves but God is faithful to help us when we cry out to Him.

We won't grow in the Christian life if we neglect our relationship with God. The writer of Haggai 1:7 declares, "This is what the Lord Almighty says, 'Give careful thought to your ways.' " Most people who come to me for counseling haven't given careful thought to their ways. They've usually neglected most aspects of their relationship with God, such as prayer, scripture meditation and memorization, church attendance, and ministry involvement. We have to maintain these disciplines if we want to have a vital, growing faith.

If we're not living in obedience to Christ, we can't expect His blessings on our lives. Jesus said it simply, "If you love me, keep my commandments." We read these assuring words in Psalm 34:17: "The righteous cry out and the Lord hears them; He delivers them from all their troubles."

Question #5 – Is this situation forcing me to cry out to God for His help and wisdom? _____

God's *help* is His faithfulness to keep our heads above water when we feel like our problems could drag us under, emotionally and physically. God's *wisdom* is His answer to the question, "How can I handle this problem and where do I go from here?" Many verses in the Bible refer to Believers who cry out to God in the midst of their trials and hardships. A counselee once did a word search for the words "cry out" on a computer Bible program. She wrote fifteen, single-spaced pages of verses that refer to crying out to God.

I love having the opportunity to comfort our children when they need their dad.

Our ten children range in age from eight to 26 years. It seems at least one or two of the younger ones get hurt every day. Many days when I return home from work, I have the privilege of comforting the little boy or girl who happened to have been wounded that day. I remember one instance in particular. Little Noelle had scraped her elbow playing street hockey, and as I sat in our living room rocking chair, holding her on my lap, I asked her to tell me all about what happened to her that day.

Even though the accident had taken place hours earlier tears trickled down her cheeks as she recalled the awful details. I hugged and kissed her and told her how sorry I was that she had gotten hurt. In those precious moments, I assured her that I cared about the pain she had gone through. She needed her daddy's comfort and sympathy.

When we experience trials, we need God in a way unlike our need for Him when our lives are going smoothly. It delights the Lord when we cry out to Him for comfort and encouragement.

God may send trials into our lives to purify us and to replace undesirable things with good things.

God uses our difficulties to purge certain things from our lives that are displeasing to Him. He also uses our trials to increase our spiritual fruitfulness. Sometimes God must "blast before He builds." We should understand that no matter what our problems are, whether we think we deserve them or not, we must cry out to the Lord in our distress. He wants our faith to result in His praise and glory as we walk in obedience to Him.

God doesn't require His children to live with intense trials every day of their lives. He sometimes takes us to a spiritual mountaintop where He grants us wonderful times of respite and refreshment. When we return to the valley, as we inevitably do, we can be confident that He's there with us also. The majesty and grandeur of the spiritual mountaintop is a nurturing and memorable experience. Yet, the time we spend with God in the valley forges a dimension of our relationship with Him that would not occur if we remained on the mountaintop.

Anyone who has been born again by faith in Christ qualifies as "the righteous."

God assures us in His Word that He hears the righteous when they cry out and He delivers them from all their troubles. "The righteous" is not a reference to a special classification of Christians. When someone becomes a part of God's family through faith in Jesus Christ, God clothes him with His robe of righteousness.

Calamity may come upon us either by "the sword of judgment," when we've done something wrong, or by "plague or famine," when we've done nothing to deserve calamity.

Our family visited friends in Miami, Florida several years ago, shortly after Hurricane Andrew had ripped through the city, and we witnessed the widespread destruction the devastating weather had caused. The hurricane didn't bypass Christians to lash its fury on unbelievers. Anyone who was in its dangerous path risked injury and loss.

Christians should never hesitate to cry out to God in times of distress.

God wants us to understand that no matter what our problems are, whether we deserve them or not, we should cry out to Him in our distress. He will hear us and save us. God is present in the midst of our trials and He wants us to have confidence that when we cry out to Him, He will be there.

The writer of 1 Peter 1:6,7 exhorts us: "In this you greatly rejoice, though now for a little while you may have had to suffer grief in all kinds of trials. These have come so that your faith—of greater worth than gold, which perishes even though refined by fire—may result in praise, glory, and honor when Jesus Christ is revealed."

Question #6 – Is God using this situation to purify my faith? Is He taking certain undesirable things out of my life and replacing them with good things? _____

God may be using the trials we're facing to make us a more effective witness for Him.

We know that God uses our trials to purge certain things from our lives that aren't pleasing to Him. If, on the other hand, we possess some excellent qualities in small measures, God may use our trials to increase our fruitfulness in His kingdom. Often, God must "blast before He can build." Just as a builder goes through the process of laying a firm foundation before he builds a house, God desires to establish a solid foundation in our lives. This foundation will enable us to honorably fulfill our biblical responsibilities. The Lord wants our faith to result in His praise and glory, both "when Jesus Christ is revealed," and now, as we walk in obedience to Him. He wants to reveal His holy character through us every day in our attitudes, our actions, and our ministries to other people.

Rather than giving us instant solutions to our problems, God builds patience into our lives.

The only way we can learn to persevere in faith is by welcoming trials into our lives. Hope is having confidence that God is in control of every detail of our life. It's being certain He will work out every problem we face for our good, and for His glory. One practical way we can learn to rejoice in our tribulations is to learn to evaluate how God develops our character through pain and suffering.

One practical way that we can learn to "greatly rejoice" in our trials and hardships is by learning the skill of evaluating God's character development in our lives. Knowing that God uses our suffering to build our character, we should prayerfully discern which character qualities God is building into our lives with each specific trial we encounter.

When we're discouraged about a situation, God wants to replace our discouragement with hope. This doesn't mean He will assure a hurting wife, for example, that if she fulfills her biblical responsibilities in the home, her husband will be the nurturing spiritual leader she wants him to be. It doesn't mean God will guarantee a frustrated teenager that if he is obedient, his parents will be compassionate and realistic in their expectations. Instead, hope is having confidence that God is in control of every detail of our lives. Hope is being certain that He will work out every problem we face, for our good and for His Glory.

Ask God for patience, and for all the other character qualities that appear in Scripture.

Few Christians today possess the virtue of patience. We tend to grow irritable and short-tempered very quickly in a stressful situation. But if we ask Him to, God promises to replace our irritability with patience. I often hear counselees say, "I don't pray for patience any more." The truth is, God will send us trials and tribulations whether we're praying for patience or not. If we don't pray for patience and the other character qualities listed in the Bible, it's unlikely that we'll respond properly to those trials when they occur in our lives.

Determination and endurance are two of the most important qualities a Christian can pursue. We sometimes become faint-hearted, and we're tempted to give up and quit when hardships arise. The only way we can learn to endure is by welcoming trials and difficulties into our lives.

The Olympic gold medallist confided in me that the last 10 miles of the day were the hardest.

One of my counseling interns won an Olympic Gold Medal several years ago. One day I asked him to describe his training schedule to me. He told me that each morning he ran seven miles before breakfast. He then ate a high protein breakfast and did weight training with other athletes for the rest of the morning. In the afternoon, he did his event training, the high jump, and then finished up each evening with a 10-mile run. He said that the 10-mile run was the hardest part of his training. By that time each day his body was nearly depleted of strength and energy, and he ran that final, torturous stretch on sheer will power. The result was that he became a world-class athlete who won a gold medal in the high jump event.

The analogy for Christians is obvious. We have a race to run and God tells us in His Word, to run that race with our hearts set on winning. We have a war to fight and God wants to equip us with the skills, resources, knowledge, and character we need to win the war. We should invite the Holy Spirit to remove those things from our lives that aren't pleasing to our heavenly Father. He will replace them with the things that bring Him glory and honor.

If we don't live according to biblical priorities our works will not be pleasing to the Lord.

God wants us to live our lives according to balanced biblical priorities. In our daily routines, we sometimes tend to stray from the scriptural priorities we've established in our lives. We easily get caught up in doing good things. God often uses trials and hardships to motivate us to accomplish the best things—not merely the good things. We should regularly re-evaluate our schedules, our goals, and our activities in light of His Word. We can't expect to live successful Christian lives if we rearrange God's order of priorities.

God has a "quality-control" program to test our work.

The writer of 1 Corinthians 3:14,15 explains: "It will be revealed with fire, and the fire will test the quality of each man's work. If what he has built survives, he will receive his reward. If it is burned up, he will suffer loss; he himself will be saved."

Question #7 – Is God using my trial to test the quality of my life? Am I living each day according to balanced biblical priorities? _____

The Lord lovingly refines our character by burning the dross out of our lives.

The first time gold goes through the fire, ninety percent of the impurities are burned out. But before gold can be classified as pure, it must go through the fire six more times. In the same way that fire refines gold, God uses trials and heartaches to purify us. He faithfully builds into our lives the holy, righteous character of His Son Jesus Christ. The 1 Corinthians 3 passage refers not primarily to a heavenly reward, but to God's sanctifying process while we're here on earth. God wants us to have the right kind of actions, attitudes, and responses toward others. The "reward" spoken of in verse 14, is God's reward of joy, peace, and contentment. These qualities constitute genuine happiness for a Christian, as He walks daily with the Lord.

The last phrase in the passage encourages us: "He himself will be saved." If the quality of our work doesn't survive God's fire, we will not lose our salvation. Rather, we lose the joy of our salvation and we forfeit many of the benefits that Christ provided for us when He died on the cross.

Have you been spiritually derailed? Is God using the trials you're presently facing to cause you to prayerfully reconsider your priorities? Scripture clearly teaches that our first priority should be our relationship with the Lord. God wants His children to spend time alone with Him on a regular basis. We need to set aside time to cultivate a consistent, meaningful prayer time, through praise, confession, petition, and intercession. And if we want to be like our heavenly Father, we must immerse ourselves in His Word.

If we're married, our spouse is our second priority. If we have children, they are our third priority. Our jobs, our church involvement, our ministries, and other activities fall in line behind these first three. When we try to rearrange this order into any other configuration, we inevitably encounter problems. While it's a simple matter to list these priorities as our goals, it's not as easy to faithfully live by them. Regularly re-evaluate your schedule, your goals, and your activities in light of His Word. Then ask God for the grace to make a renewed commitment to live according to His priorities.

Often our most meaningful ministries grow out of our greatest weaknesses.

Sometimes God uses our trials to prepare us for a ministry of helping others. He always proves Himself strong in our weakness and humiliation. God has the power to solve our problems when we are utterly powerless to help ourselves. I've often told counselees that I wish I could share with them a dynamic Christian testimony of personal strength and success. But the truth is, my counseling ministry has grown out of my failures. I have failed in my personal life, my marriage, and my ministry. In spite of my unworthiness, God has faithfully granted me His grace, extended me His forgiveness, and brought about reconciliation in situations that once seemed hopeless.

My counseling ministry grows out of my weakness and God's strength.

God has proven Himself strong in my weakness and humiliation. I am personally acquainted with the heartache and pain that most of my counselees experience. I know, firsthand, God's power to solve our problems when we are powerless to help ourselves. One of my greatest joys is to offer the same biblical comfort to hurting people that I myself have received.

Many counselees who come to me are so discouraged by their circumstances that they've given up all hope of ever being whole again. As I open up my heart to them and describe the glorious way God has rebuilt my once-shattered life, I have, on countless occasions, seen their despair give way to gresh hope in the Lord. I have the privilege of encouraging them with the comfort with which I have been comforted.

Although we may find it hard to believe, God wants to comfort other hurting people through our lives.

We may be unable to envision a time when our present trials will be a source of hope and encouragement to someone who is suffering. Yet, when we learn to respond biblically to our problems, God will use us to minister to other hurting people. The writer of 2 Corinthians 1:3-5 states: "Praise be to the God and Father of our Lord Jesus Christ, the Father of compassion and the God of all comfort, Who comforts us in all our troubles, so that we can comfort those in any trouble with the comfort we ourselves have received from God. For just as the sufferings of Christ flow over into our lives, so also through Christ, our comfort overflows."

Question #8 – Is God using this trial to prepare me for a ministry of comforting and helping other people?

_____

Do you truly want to know Christ, as the Apostle Paul described, in His power and in His suffering? Until you learn to respond to your problems in the right way, you won't derive the benefits God has planned for His children who endure suffering.

Job maintained his confidence in God throughout his time of testing.

When Job was overcome with an avalanche of trials and tribulations, he faithfully declared, "Though He slay me, yet I will hope in Him...Indeed, this will turn out for my deliverance." He knew he would be a better person as a result of his trials. The mature man that we find at the end of the Book of Job is very different than the untested righteous man that we meet at the beginning of the book.

Question #9 – Is God allowing me to go through this situation so that I will learn to glorify Him with a right response to trials and hardships? _____

Chapter 16

The High Cost of Bitterness

We can't hide unresolved bitterness. It exhausts us mentally, physically, and spiritually.

When we harbor resentment against someone, certain glands in our bodies, including the pituitary, thyroid, and adrenal glands, produce excessive amounts of hormones. These hormones can cause a breakdown in any part of our body. A refusal to forgive can also cause depression, insomnia, chronic fatigue, and anxiety attacks. This chapter profiles the story of a 75-year old woman who underwent six years of drug therapy in an attempt to remedy her unwillingness to forgive.

Forgiveness Principle #8: We must understand the physical, spiritual, and emotional consequences that occur when we maintain hurt feelings.

Bitterness and unforgiveness take their toll on every part of our body. When we refuse to forgive an offender, our face takes on a look of hardness. Although we may try to conceal the resentment we feel toward others, it soon etches itself into our eyes and our facial muscles. Our countenance then permanently reflects our inner bitterness.

When unresolved bitterness resides in our hearts, it shows. We can't hide it. Few competent physicians would deny that pent-up bitterness can lead to physical problems such as ulcerative colitis, toxic goiters, high blood pressure, anxiety attacks, and headaches.

People who refuse to forgive their offenders often feel drained and exhausted.

Someone who refuses to forgive may also experience physical fatigue. Many people today are diagnosed with Chronic Fatigue Syndrome. While I certainly don't believe that everyone who suffers from Chronic Fatigue harbors unresolved bitterness in their hearts, I think for some people, the possibility may worthy of consideration.

Sleep deprivation is often another consequence of unresolved bitterness. Sleep loss produces such symptoms as hallucinations, paranoia, and bizarre behavior. Some of the strangest situations that I've dealt with over the years have been related to sleep deprivation, and prescription and illegal drugs.

Her psychiatric consultations lasted ten minutes and cost $125 dollars per session.

One day a 75-year-old woman came to me for counseling because she was depressed. For six years, she'd been under the care of a psychiatrist. He saw her every other week for a 10-minute session and he charged her $125 dollars per appointment. Her husband resented the fact that they were paying this doctor to do nothing more than regulate her medication. The psychiatrist gave her no counseling whatsoever. She came to me because she was still depressed after six years of drug therapy. When she decided to make an appointment with me her husband reacted angrily. "He's another one of those doctors who's going to take your money and not do you a bit of good!" he cautioned her. I understood why he felt that way.

They each had their own remote control and they were more like roommates than marriage partners.

She seemed perfectly normal the first time I met with her. She told me that she and her husband were having marriage problems. They'd been married for 30 years and had both been previously widowed. She explained they had gotten married for the sake of convenience. She had her own bedroom and he had his. She had her remote control and he had his. She had stopped preparing meals for him years earlier. But they faithfully attended church as a couple. They drove separate vehicles but they sat together during the worship service. When I asked her why they sat together, she responded indignantly, "Well, Dr. Dunlap, we don't want anyone thinking there's something wrong with our marriage!" As I listened to her story, I knew my work was cut out for me.

Depression and sleep deprivation can cause a person to hallucinate and appear to be paranoid.

This elderly woman, who'd been taking antidepressant medication for years before coming for counseling, had not slept for several days and was severely depressed. She was convinced her relatives had inserted an electronic monitoring device in her nose. She said her husband was trying to commit her to a mental hospital, and she even believed her pastor was in on the conspiracy against her. She was desperate for help.

My first session with "Mrs. Everette," had been very productive. She related details of her troubled marriage and we discussed a program to gradually decrease her antidepressant medication.

She handed me the box of documents and told me about the plot that her family had formed against her.

On the morning of her second appointment she was visibly upset when she walked into my office. She made her way to my desk and handed me a large cardboard box. "These," she announced, "are all my important papers." As I glanced through the contents of the box I saw various documents such as her will, her insurance papers, and her appliance warranties. "You're the only person I trust," she informed me. "They're trying to prove I'm mentally incompetent so they can put me in a psychiatric hospital and take my house away from me." Then she asked me if I would agree to take care of the box for her.

She said her 88 year-old husband was trying to commit her to a mental hospital.

I sat the box on the floor and asked her to be seated. "Who's trying to prove you're mentally incompetent?" I questioned her. "My husban's in on it," she replied, "and his children are in on it." Her husband was 88 years old and his children were all between 50 and 60 years old. She continued, "The next door neighbor's in on it, and the postman's in on it too." At this point she reached into her purse and pulled out a cassette tape. "Dr. Dunlap," she said, "if you'll listen to this tape, you'll see my preacher is also in on it."

She believed family members had put an electronic bug in her nose.

Then she made a startling revelation. "There's one other thing you need to know. They came into my room in the middle of the night this past week and put an electronic bug in my nose so they can monitor my conversations," she confided in a voice barely above a whisper. "An electronic bug in your nose?" I asked her incredulously. "I knew you wouldn't believe me," she countered, "so I brought it to show you." Well I enjoy little electronic gadgets, so I said, "That would be fine, Mrs. Everette. I would like to see it."

She slowly pulled a tissue out of her purse. It had been folded over and secured with a small piece of tape.

She opened it up to make certain the contents were still there. Then she confidently folded it back up and handed it to me. There I was, sitting in my office chair, carefully opening up this tissue so I wouldn't drop whatever was in it. And sure enough, there was something in it. It looked exactly like something that had come out of someone's nose. She was thoroughly convinced it was an electronic bug.

I've frequently dealt with paranoid people. Sometimes in the midst of moments like these, God grants special grace and wisdom. I was working with a Christian physician at that time and he had a powerful microscope in his medical laboratory. So I told her, "Mrs. Everette, I want our lab technician to take a look at this under our microscope so we can verify exactly what it is. Would that be OK with you?" She agreed it would be fine and cautioned me to be careful not to drop it. As I excused myself to walk out to the lab and stall for a little time, I prayed God would show me how to offer this woman biblical help and encouragement.

The lab technician was somewhat surprised to see what was in the tissue.

After I obtained her permission to view the evidence under our microscope, I asked the lab technician if I could speak with her for a moment. I told her, "My counselee believes this tissue contains an electronic bug. Would you look at this under the microscope and tell me if you see any microscopic electronic components?" A doctor and a nurse were standing nearby consulting a patient's file. They stopped their conversation and began to listen to me as I informed the lab technician of what had transpired with Mrs. Everette. They jokingly told me later on that day that when they first overheard me talking about the electronic nose bug they thought I might need to take a little time off for some rest and relaxation.

She placed it on the slide and focused the microscope, but saw no electronic components.

The technician focused the microscope and said, "I can assure you that there are no electronic components here." She invited me to take a look, and then she took it off the slide and put it back into the tissue. I returned to my office and informed Mrs. Everette that she had brought me nothing more than dried up mucus from her nose. She buried her face in her hands and cried, "Maybe I *am* going crazy, Dr. Dunlap. They probably *should* have me committed!"

Her husband's children told her she would soon have to find another place to live.

I asked her to describe what had taken place in the seven days since we'd last seen each other. I told her I hadn't observed any agitation or paranoia in our first meeting. She explained that a few days earlier she and her husband had gone to his son's home for Sunday lunch. All three of her husband's children and spouses were there. When the eight of them had finished their meal the oldest son turned directly to her and stately flatly, "We want you both to know that when Dad dies we plan to sell the house you're living in and divide the profits among ourselves. You'll have to make arrangements to live somewhere else. We all grew up in that house and we consider it our inheritance."

Mr. Everette had nearly died the month before from an aneurysm. These children were telling their 75-year-old stepmother they would one day evict her from the home she had lived in for 30 years. She had helped to purchase the home. When she married her husband 30 years earlier, she had sold her first home and used all her equity to pay off the mortgage on their present home.

The encounter with her stepchildren had devastated her. It was now obvious to me how she had reached the emotional state she was presently in. During that appointment I began to teach her the principles of biblical forgiveness and she responded to the truths as enthusiastically as anyone I've ever counseled.

Several months later, after we'd worked through the principles of biblical forgiveness, Mrs. Everette looked like a different person. One day I walked to the waiting room to call her name for her appointment. The waiting room was particularly crowded that morning. When I looked around and couldn't find her, I returned to my office for a moment.

Her face looked so different that I didn't even recognize her.

I came out a second time and once again surveyed all the patients. When I didn't see her, I asked the receptionist if Mrs. Everett had signed in for her appointment. She checked the sign-in sheet and said she had, indeed, signed her name.

She was seated on the waiting room loveseat, beside her 88 year-old husband.

Then I spotted her. She was seated beside a man on a love seat in the far corner of the waiting room. She had been there for at least fifteen minutes. I hadn't recognized her because she had a beautiful, radiant smile on her face. I'd never seen her smile before. Her countenance was entirely changed.

When I walked over to greet her she introduced me to her husband and told me he wanted to meet with me. I remembered the comment he had made weeks earlier, "Just another one of those doctors who's only interested in your money." I invited them to come back to my office and she said, "No Dr. Dunlap, he wants to meet with you *alone.*"

I kept a cautious eye on the cane her husband was carrying.

As we were walking to my office I wondered if I should alert one of my colleagues to keep an ear out for me. I've dealt with many irate men and women during the past several years but this man had a *cane* in his hand. Of course, the fact that he was 88 years old was consoling. I figured I could probably outrun him!

When we reached my office and sat down, he hadn't even gotten settled in the chair before he leaned forward, pointed his finger in my face, and said, "Young man, I don't know what you've done to my wife, but whatever it is you better keep it up!" "Well, sir," I replied, "she and I have almost finished the counseling process. I think we've dealt with her wrong attitudes, and we've discussed her root problems and how she should handle them." Mrs. Everette had gone to her husband several weeks earlier to ask for his forgiveness for the many times she'd offended him throughout the years of their marriage.

He couldn't believe the change he had witnessed in his wife. He told me, "I don't care if *you* think you're done with her. I want her to keep coming to see you until *I* say she's done." He wanted to be certain she didn't slip back into her old habits.

Mrs. Everette came to see me once a quarter for the next four years. Our final session was quite emotional because of the bond of mutual love and respect that had grown between us. By this time, she was 79 years old and her husband was 92. She thanked me for being God's instrument to teach her how to live to His glory. She then said there was one thing more she wanted to thank me for. She told me that since she'd begun counseling with me, she and her husband had experienced a degree of fulfillment in their marriage that they'd never previously shared. She said, "Dr. Dunlap, I want you to know that during these past four years we've had the best sex we've ever had in our lives!"

As I sat there, a little uncertain as to how I should respond, her laughter relieved the momentary awkwardness. I told her that her news greatly encouraged me and gave me something to look forward to in my own marriage. She was living proof that we can maintain our joy and marital satisfaction as we grow older. As long as we're willing to walk in loving obedience to the Lord, His hand of blessing will rest faithfully upon our lives.

If we harbor resentment in our heart, we can't love God as we should, or minister effectively to others.

I recently read an interesting front-page article in our local newspaper on rheumatoid arthritis. The journalist explained the correlation between emotions and the onset of arthritis. He went on to provide documentation to support the claim that stress, worry, and anxiety make the body vulnerable to arthritis, which attacks the joints and the bones.

The writer of Leviticus 17:11 tells us: "the life of the flesh is in the blood." Interestingly, the marrow of our bones is the "factory" that produces our blood. The health of our bones, therefore, determines our body's health. Bitterness has a direct and devastating effect on our bones. Consider these words from Proverbs 17:22: "A cheerful heart is good medicine, but a crushed spirit dries up the bones."

When we harbor resentment against someone, we can't possibly love God as we should.

When we resent someone, we're unable to love God. 1 John 4:20,21 warns: "If a man says, 'I love God,' and hates his brother, he is a liar: for he that loves not his brother whom he has seen, how can he love God whom he has not seen? And this commandment we have from Him, that he who loves God loves his brother also." Resentment is almost always accompanied by doubts regarding our relationship with God.

A resentful spirit hinders us from ministering to other people effectively.

When we repeat the Lord's Prayer we ask God to forgive our trespasses in the same way that we forgive people who trespass against us. We can't minister effectively to people when we harbor unforgivness in our hearts. When they sense our attitude of resentment, as they inevitably will, they will resist whatever spiritual truths we're trying to communicate to them. Case study #9 is an example of a man whose family resisted his ministry in their lives because he had unforgiveness in his heart.

His wife announced that she wanted a divorce and that she wasn't interested in reconciling.

He was a very successful pastor who had started a church with four couples. Within six years, the church had grown to more than 700 in attendance. They built a worship center and paid cash for it. He was a dynamic, effective teacher and a nurturing pastor. People were coming to salvation weekly and church members were growing in their relationship with Christ. He was stunned when his wife told him one day that she wanted a divorce, she was taking the children, and she was not open to the possibility of reconciliation.

He hadn't picked up on a single cue that his marriage was in trouble.

He had no idea, whatsoever, that any problem had existed in their marriage. They had three children, ages 13, 11, and 7, and he thought his family was perfectly happy. His wife explained her reason for leaving. She told him, "You're married to the ministry. It is your wife, your mistress, and your children."

She continued, "You've had 15 years to change and I haven't seen you make a single effort to do so." This man had plunged, practically overnight, from the pinnacle of success to the abyss of despair. I was confident, however, that he would find help and hope as he learned to apply the biblical principles of forgiveness to his seemingly hopeless situation.

His wife kept everything to herself and never told her husband how she felt about their relationship.

His wife was the kind of person who kept her feelings inside. She had never expressed to him the slightest discontentment or displeasure in their relationship. Instead, she quietly came to a breaking point. She left her husband and took their three children with her. He was devastated. The church was devastated. They gave him six months to attempt to reconcile with her. She divorced him as soon as she legally could and he resigned from his position as pastor. When he came to me for counseling a few months later, he sat before me weeping.

This man who had a seminary degree in theology told me he doubted whether he was even a Christian. As we began the counseling process it soon became obvious to me that his problem was not that he was unsaved. His problem was the hurt and bitterness he had allowed to accumulate in his heart throughout the years. Now he felt resentful toward God because he believed God had taken away not only his wife and children, but his ministry as well.

Even though he hadn't lived by biblical priorities, he still believed the divorce was his wife's fault.

This man resigned his pastorate because he he'd been living by wrong priorities. He'd disqualified himself from ministry because he had failed to manage his own household. His wife's request for a divorce didn't cause the trial he was facing. He was stuck in a "victim mentality" when he came to see me. He felt very sorry for himself and told me that his wife had "dealt him a sorry hand."

He was using his children as pawns to try to make his wife feel guilty. He would tell them how horribly he was doing. Then he would launch into a complaint session and blame their mom for all the misery he was going through. He gradually alienated his children to the point that they didn't even want to visit him on the weekends. They knew he would just bombard them with emotional manipulation.

He understood for the first time that God was in sovereign control of his problems.

As we worked through the forgiveness principles, he began to see that he was not a victim. He began to understand that God had providentially allowed these problems to come into his life. He asked God to forgive him for his sins of unbelief and selfishness. Then he repented for the all the years he had lived by wrong priorities. He also confessed the unforgiveness and bitterness that he had maintained for years toward various people who had offended him throughout his life.

This pastor asked his children to forgive him and he purposed, by God's grace, to not speak negatively again to them about their mother. He humbled himself before his ex-wife and asked for her forgiveness, but she refused to forgive him. She told him that for years she'd been accustomed to living as a single parent and she wanted no further contact with him.

But his three children forgave him and they witnessed the miraculous effects of the principles of biblical forgiveness in their father's life. Today, they continue to share a wonderful relationship that's based on the all sufficient grace of God.

Chapter 17

Attentiveness to My Offender's Needs

God gives us a window of opportunity to minister Christ's love to people who offend us.

Christians must learn to view each offense committed against them, as God's way of drawing attention to the offender's needs. God uses offenses to give us an open door into the offender's life. Jesus is our supreme example of this kind of forgiveness, as we see in His prayer in Luke 23:24: "Father, forgive them, for they do not know what they are doing." God will grant us the grace to resolve our resentment and to discern whatever emotional, spiritual, or material need may have motivated our offender to hurt us. Then we should take steps to minister to his needs.

Depression and anxiety are two of the most significant consequences of refusing to forgive the people who offend us. God places His hand of discipline upon His children who refuse to obey Him. When we live in a depressed, anxious state, it soon becomes impossible for us to think clearly.

He was so angry with his wife that he would become disoriented to the point of not knowing where he was.

Our reasoning ability, power of concentration and memory are all adversely affected when we choose to maintain hurt feelings. One man who came to me for counseling was very distraught that his wife had asked him to leave. He owned a multi-million dollar business and he drove hundreds of miles each week on business trips. When he and his wife first separated, he was so angry and depressed that he would forget where he was.

He would have to exit off the Interstate, ask someone to explain where he was, and figure out how to get home ao he could regain his composure enough to head out again for his business meeting. His hostility and anger toward his wife severely affected his reasoning ability.

Forgiveness Principle #9: We must learn to view an offense as God's way of drawing our attention to the offender's needs.

When we take steps to pray for our offender and minister to his needs, we make measurable progress in the process of biblical forgiveness.

I listed all the things my wife did to irritate me.

Three months after I got married, I realized my wife and I were in serious trouble. One evening we had a heated argument and I was very angry. I sat down afterwards and did a typically male thing. I made a list of 17 things I didn't like about my wife. These were things about her that frustrated me. I listed several attitudes I didn't care for and certain personality traits that irritated

me. Now I was smart enough to know it would be unwise to leave this list lying around. So I took it to my office, put it in my filing cabinet, and in a few days, completely forgot about it.

God disciplined our stubbornness until we were willing to admit that we needed help.

About four years later, we had the worst conflict we'd ever experienced. When God brought us to the point of being willing to humble ourselves, we went to see a counselor. In time, God granted us the healing we desperately needed in our lives and in our marriage.

One day as I was thumbing through some folders in my file cabinet I came across the list I had made years earlier. I was surprised and encouraged as I read through the 17 things I had written. I realized that God had radically changed 14 of those 17 aspects of my wife's life. And He had changed even more things in my own life. I wish I'd known at the time I wrote the list, how God uses offenses in our lives to give us opportunities to minister to our offenders. Then I would've fervently and consistently prayed for those 17 needs in my wife's life, instead of whining about them to the Lord.

When I found the list that day, I thanked God that although I had failed to respond biblically to my wife's offenses, He had mercifully granted us restoration and reconciliation.

Chapter 18

She Forgave a Murderer

We must forgive our offenders before God, but we don't tell them we forgive them unless they ask us to.

In this chapter we meet a woman counselee who was full of grief and bitterness. An irate neighbor had shot and killed her husband, and he died before the ambulance arrived. She was seething with hatred for her neighbor and consumed with resentment toward God. After learning the principles of biblical forgiveness she forgave the murderer. She calmly took the witness stand in the courtroom and related the necessary facts in a way that was free of anger and hostility.

Forgiveness Principle #10: Biblical forgiveness has both vertical and horizontal dimensions.

Many Christians don't understand Forgiveness Principle #10. However, a Believer who wants to learn how to forgive biblically must learn the difference between forgiving an offender face to face ("horizontal" forgiveness), and forgiving him before God ("vertical" forgiveness.)

We must be willing to forgive our offenders an infinite number of times.

Jesus instructs us in Luke 17:3,4, "If your brother sins, admonish him, and if he repents, forgive him. If he sins against you seven times a day, and seven times comes back to you and says, 'I repent,' forgive him." God wants us to understand that we're not permitted to set a limit on the number of times we'll forgive an offender who asks for our forgiveness.

We can' tell an offender that we forgive him, unless he first asks us to.

God also requires us to grant an offender immediate forgiveness in our hearts, whether or not he ever asks us for forgiveness. When we refuse to do this we allow a root of bitterness to spring up in our hearts. The bitterness will defile our lives and the lives of others as well.

We discussed this in a previous chapter, but it definitely bears repeating: We're not in a position to tell offenders we forgive them unless they first ask for our forgiveness. God hasn't authorized us to do this. This may lead them to think they are "off the hook." Unrepentant offenders are *not* off the hook with God, and, depending upon the nature of the offense, they may not be off the hook with the legal authorities.

He politely asked his neighbor to move his car off of his property.

A woman who came for counseling described a tragic event that had recently taken place in her life. It is illustrative of the two kinds of forgiveness. She was sitting on her front porch one evening with her husband and her 2 year-old son, when a neighbor drove up and parked his car on their property. Her husband expressed his displeasure and calmly asked the man to move his car. Her husband's tone of voice was not irate or threatening.

Her neighbor shot her husband and he died before the ambulance arrived.

An argument ensued and the neighbor became angry. He reached into his glove compartment, pulled out a handgun, and there, in front of the woman and her son, shot her husband. He died before the ambulance arrived. When I first met her she was one of the angriest people I'd ever dealt with. She was seething with hatred for her neighbor and full of resentment toward God. We began, immediately to work through the principles of biblical forgiveness.

A few months later, when the trial date finally arrived, she had to take the witness stand and tell the court what this neighbor had done to her husband. It was obvious to everyone in the courtroom that she was not embittered against her neighbor. She couldn't tell him, "I forgive you for murdering my husband," because he was unrepentant. He had never *asked* for her forgiveness, but she had forgiven him in her heart before God. She related the facts of the incident without demonstrating the hostility and resentment that often typify such courtroom testimonies. The people who attended the trial marveled at how calmly and graciously she conducted herself. God had done a mighty work of grace in her heart.

Chapter 19

She Heaped Burning Coals

We must cooperate with God in our offenders' lives, by serving them and ministering to their needs.

Have you ever wondered why God tells us to do good deeds for our enemies? This case study relates the story of a woman who lost her job when jealous co-workers lied about her to her employer. Convinced that her enthusiasm made them look bad, they devised a plan to get her fired. She was so resentful and bitter toward them that she began to have severe anxiety and chest pains. When her physician couldn't find anything physically wrong with her, he recommended counseling where she began to learn the principles of biblical forgiveness.

Thus far, we've learned ten principles of biblical forgiveness. Let's examine the next principle of forgiveness.

Forgiveness Principle #11: We must cooperate with God in our offender's life.

Counselees often get as far as Forgiveness Principle #11 and refuse to budge. God instructs us to feed our enemies if they're hungry. If they're thirsty we should give them something to drink. In other words, God holds us responsible for doing good deeds for our enemies.

I've counseled many people throughout the years who've been unwilling to obey this scriptural command. They apply all the other forgiveness principles to their lives but they stop short of being willing to perform acts of kindness for their offenders. They don't understand that the resentment remaining in their heart—because of their refusal to obey this command—hinders their spiritual growth.

Her coworkers called her "Little Miss Enthusiastic" behind her back.

"Julie" was referred to me for counseling after her employer had unjustly fired her from her job as secretary in a physician's office.

She was energetic and enthusiastic—a classic "Type A" personality. She would come to work thirty minutes early, work through her lunch break and work thirty minutes late at the end of the day. She loved her job and she never expected extra compensation for her hard work.

They never invited Julie to join their outings.

Three other women worked in the same office with her. They had been there for several years before Julie was hired and they were all good friends. They partied together, ate lunch together and vacationed together, but they never invited Julie to come along. They believed her diligence and enthusiasm made them look bad and they considered her a threat.

What made matters even worse was the fact that Julie was blessed with a great metabolism. Even though she snacked on French pastries and Coke each morning during coffee break, she never gained weight. The other three ladies, all overweight, glowered at her enviously while they snacked on carrot sticks and water.

They were determined Julie wouldn't be their supervisor, so they hatched a plan.

When the physicians announced they were planning to hire an office manager, none of the three friends wanted the job. Not one of them wanted to supervise her friends. Their friendship meant more to them than a small increase in salary. As you may have already guessed, Julie applied for the job.

In an effort to prevent Julie from getting the promotion, they secretly altered some of her computer work to make it appear that she'd lost several thousand dollars' worth of patients' payments. They hid the corresponding paperwork so the accusation couldn't be disproved. The doctors fired Julie and within two weeks she was admitted to the hospital with chest pains. She thought she was having a heart attack.

When her physician couldn't find anything physically wrong with her, he referred Julie to me. Within a few minutes of our initial meeting I detected her deep hurt and resentment toward her former work associates who had mistreated her. We began immediately to discuss the principles of biblical forgiveness.

Several weeks later when we came to the final principle, I told her

I wanted her to design a plan for doing an anonymous good deed for the three women at the office. I could tell by the look of shock on her face that she was *not* thrilled with my suggestion.

When I asked Julie to think of some practical act of kindness she could do for her three former work associates she was stunned. "You're telling me I have to do something *good* for those women?" she shouted in amazement. "They got me fired! They sabotaged my computer and lied about me! I don't want to have anything to do with them. I never want to *see* them again, and I'm not about to do anything nice for them!" She folded her arms resolutely and sat back in her chair with a very determined look on her face.

I told her she would be resentful toward her former co-workers until she obeyed God's command in Romans 12.

I read her the verses once more from Romans 12: "Bless those who persecute you...never pay back evil for evil to anyone...If your enemy is hungry, feed him, and if he is thirsty, give him a drink...overcome evil with good." I explained that she couldn't fully forgive the three women who had persecuted her until she did something good for them. I also reminded her that she would never truly be free of hurt and anger until she complied with *all* of God's requirements for forgiveness.

Julie soon decided she would obey God's command, and together we designed a project. There was a bakery shop located next door to the physicians' office. She phoned the manager and arranged to have fresh bagels and low-fat muffins delivered anonymously to the women one morning a week, for six weeks. She later reported to me that the fifty dollars she spent on the project was the best investment she'd ever made. Her willingness to take the final step in biblical forgiveness freed her from the bitterness and resentment that had filled her heart.

I soon learned she was also having problems with her husband and her daughter.

Yet, that's not where the story ends. As we continued the counseling process I discovered that Julie and her husband had been experiencing marriage problems for several years. He had been unwilling to get outside help until he saw the miraculous change in his wife's attitude. Their teenage daughter was also having problems. She was rebelling against their authority, engaging in self-destructive behavior, and beginning to get into serious trouble at school.

Eventually, Julie's husband and her daughter began to come with her for counseling. Her husband was eager to deal biblically with the offenses he had committed against his wife and daughter. They told me their marriage would have soon ended in divorce if they hadn't come for counseling. They agreed that their daughter would have been unreachable within another six months.

She found a job that was much better than her previous one.

God gloriously restored their family. They joined a solid, Bible-believing church and started attending regularly. Julie found a new job working for Christian physicians in a spiritually encouraging environment, earning a much higher salary. They appreciated her enthusiasm and rewarded her diligence. One of the physician's wives led a weekly Bible study for the office staff members and Julie began to grow in her Christian walk in a way she never had before.

Her life is a demonstration of the blessings that God has in store for His children who are willing to follow Him, rather than their own natural inclinations, no matter what the personal cost to themselves may be.

Chapter 20

Practical Steps to Forgive an Offender

Christians must repent and seek God's forgiveness for their unwillingness to forgive others.

As we arrive at the actual process of forgiveness, we'll consider six practical steps that guide us in the process of biblically forgiving offenders. Before we discuss the six steps, however, you must first understand what it means to be willing to forgive someone who has hurt you. If you decide you are willing to work through the principles of biblical forgiveness, you should agree to the following five commitments before you begin the actual process of forgiving your offenders.

This preliminary checklist will help us prepare to go through the steps of biblical forgiveness.

#1 – Do I agree that I'll never again bring up the offense to use against my offender? (It's an unfair tactic.) _____

#2 – Am I willing to consciously and deliberately forgive the offenses that were committed against me? (This involves writing them down, so I can deal with them specifically and individually.) _____

#3 – Am I willing to give thanks to God in the midst of this process, recognizing that He has sovereignly allowed these offenses to occur? (I'm not thanking God *for* the offenses, but for His good and overriding purposes in allowing these offenses to take place.) _____

#4 – Do I agree to do good deeds for those people who have wronged me? (I acknowledge the fact that I'll be unable to successfully complete the forgiveness process if I'm unwilling to do good deeds for them.) _____

#5 – Am I willing to discern the ongoing good that God will continue to bring out of this situation? (I realize that as I work through these steps, I'll gain a progressively clearer understanding of why God has allowed me to go through these trials and

☐

hardships.) _____

Now we're ready to move on to the practical steps of biblical forgiveness. After reviewing the preparatory checklist above, if you decide you truly want to forgive the people who have offended you, you should proceed to work through the following six steps of biblical forgiveness. Ask a trustworthy Christian friend to sit with you as you work through these steps. It could be your pastor, a family member, or an accountability or prayer partner. But it's very important that you do *not* go through this process alone.

Step #1 – Ask God to forgive you for your lack of forgiveness.

An unwillingness to forgive is a sin against the Holy Spirit. You must begin by humbly and prayerfully submitting yourself to God in repentance for your lack of forgiveness.

Step #2 – Make a list of the people who have hurt you.

There is only one legitimate reason for writing an extensive list of other people's offenses against you—to use it as a tool to focus your attention on specifically forgiving your offenders. Doing it for any other reason is wrong. You should list the offenses as specifically as you possibly can. You do this to clarify the exact nature of each offense, so you can fully forgive each person individually. As you list each offense, resist the temptation to place blame or imply guilt.

This step is often very emotional for most people. I want to emphasize again the importance of having someone with you during this process to encourage you and comfort you in the Lord.

Step #3 – Consciously and deliberately forgive your offenders before God.

You should go through each offense individually and preface each statement with, "Lord I forgive." For example, "Lord, I forgive my husband for being unwilling to meet my needs." "Lord, I forgive my wife for her angry responses." "Lord, I forgive my son or daughter for his or her attitude of rebellion and disrespect."

This is only phase one of Step #3. After some time has passed, you may remember more offenses that you didn't write down on your list. People generally deal with the big offenses first, and once they are properly dealt with they may begin to think of other offenses that have occurred over the course of their lives.

Each time in the future that you remember another offense, you should bring it immediately before God. If you're alone, name the offense out loud. Be mindful of the fact that many offenses will occur on a continuing basis, especially in a marriage relationship.

This act of definitive forgiveness does not erase the need to forgive the same offenses again every time they occur. You will know you're maturing in your ability to forgive when you forgive an offender quickly, *before* you allow seething anger and resentment to lodge in your heart.

Step #4 – By faith, thank God that He intends to use each of these offenses to benefit your life.

It's important to understand that you're not thanking God for the offenses themselves, but rather for His overriding purposes for good in allowing them to take place. There should be a reservoir in your heart of thanksgiving to God when you think of the various ways He's used your trials and hardships to bestow blessings on your life.

Step #5 – Begin to think of specific ways you can serve your offenders and do good deeds for them.

Some suggestions are: praying for them, acting friendly toward them, praising their positive qualities, defending them if other people criticize them, expressing appreciation to them, or helping to alleviate some of their stress by serving them in specific ways. There are countless things you can do. You should pray that God would give you wisdom and sensitivity to do good deeds for your offenders.

In situations where sexual immorality has occurred, it would be inappropriate to send a card or flowers, for example, or to do anything that would appear suspicious to a spouse. In this type of situation, the only good you may be able to do is pray for them. Commit yourself to prayi for them regularly.

Step #6 – Consider each offense separately and ask God to reveal to you, how He used each offense to develop character in your life.

At this point I suggest you reread the section in Chapter 15, subtitled "Evaluating God's Character Development," and attempt to answer each question thoughtfully and prayerfully if you haven't already done so. These answers will help you deal positively with the memories of the offenses when they surface in your mind, as they occasionally will.

Here's a checklist to help readers evaluate God's character development program in their lives. Keep in mind, as we've discussed in earlier chapters, that God is forming the character of His Son Jesus Christ in the lives of His children. Each time we face a new trial we should remember how God uses the difficulties we encounter to produce more of Christ's character in us. Then, rather than complain about our circumstances, we should praise God for His work of grace.

We find a comforting promise in Philippians 1:6: "I am confident of this very thing, that He, Who began a good work in you, will perfect it until the day of Christ Jesus."

The following checklist has proven to be a valuable tool to many counselees. As they've encountered various trials and hardships, they have used this list to evaluate God's character development in their lives.

As you read each question, rate your answers on a scale of 1 to 10. Then identify the five character qualities you rated the highest, and memorize them. Write them on 3x5 cards and place them in strategic locations around your home and in your car, for instance, as reminders of how God is working in your life.

Each time a new conflict arises, or whenever someone or something stirs up painful memories in your mind, recall how the Lord has used your trials to produce more of His character in you. Then praise Him for His work of grace. These principles of forgiveness have the power to set you free.

FAITH or DISOBEDIENCE? Am I trusting in God and relying upon Him? Am I demonstrating obedience to the Word of God? _____

HOPE or DISCOURAGEMENT? Do I have confidence that God is in control and that He will work all things out for my good and for His glory? _____

☐

LOVE or SELFISHNESS? Do I give to the needs of others without expecting anything in return? _____

PATIENCE or IRRITABILITY? Do I willingly accept difficult situations from God as a normal part of the Christian life? Do I respond to them correctly? _____

RESPONSIBILITY or UNRELIABILITY? Do I make it my practice to both know and do what God and others are expecting from me? _____

FORGIVENESS or RESENTMENT? When someone offends me, do I acknowledge the fact that God has allowed that offense to occur? Do I take the necessary biblical steps to deal properly with the offense? _____

SELF-CONTROL or SELF-INDULGENCE? When I encounter a trial, do I instantly obey the promptings of the Holy Spirit? Do I seek to do the right thing even though the circumstances are difficult? _____

PEACE or ANXIETY? Do I structure my life around that which is eternal and cannot be destroyed or taken away? _____

GENTLENESS or ANGER? Have I yielded all my personal rights and expectations to God? _____

DETERMINATION of FAINT-HEARTEDNESS? Have I purposed to do anything that God expects of me, regardless of how difficult it may be? _____

ENDURANCE or GIVING UP? Do I possess the inward strength to withstand stress and keep going, in order to accomplish God's best? _____

JOY or SELF-PITY? Do I have an inner radiance that results from being in genuine harmony with God and with others? _____

KINDNESS or INDIFFERENCE? Do I make a habit of investing whatever time, energy, and resources are necessary to heal the hurts of others? _____

GOODNESS or IMPURITY? Does my moral character demonstrate a commitment to live my life in obedience to God's Word? _____

☐

DILIGENCE or SLOTHFULNESS? Do I visualize each task I encounter as a special assignment from the Lord? Do I use all my energies to accomplish it? _____

TOLERANCE or PREJUDICE? Do I accept other people in whatever stage of spiritual maturity they may be, without demanding them to change? _____

GRATEFULNESS or INGRATITUDE? Do I make known to God and to other people the ways in which they have benefited my life? _____

FAIRNESS or PARTIALITY? Do I try to consider a situation from the viewpoint of every person involved? _____

Chapter 21

Personal Evaluation Checklists

"A Wife's Checklist of Offenses"

Many wives deny the fact that they've allowed a root of bitterness to grow in their hearts against their husbands. For a wife to forgive her husband, she must first acknowledge and identify the offenses he has committed against her. Then she can specifically and thoroughly forgive him before God, for every one of his offenses against her.

Most women who are unhappily married are not fully aware of the specific ways their husband has offended them. They harbor general feelings of resentment in their heart toward their husband, but they're unable to determine the exact reasons why.

This checklist is intended to help women identify 123 ways husbands typically offend their wives. As you read through this list, check the items that apply to your individual situation. Then use those items as a guide to specifically forgive your husband.

I forgive my husband for:

_____1.   Ignoring me.
_____2.   Not valuing my opinions.
_____3.   Paying more attention to other people than to me.
_____4.   Not listening to me, or not understanding what I feel is important.
_____5.   Closing me out by not talking to me, or by not listening to me (the Silent Treatment.)
_____6.   Being easily distracted when I'm trying to talk with him.
_____7.   Not scheduling special time to be with me.
_____8.   Not being open to talk about things he doesn't understand.
_____9.   Not being open to talk about things I don't understand.
_____10. Not giving me a chance to fully voice my opinions on decisions that affect the entire family.
_____11. Punishing me by being angry or silent.
_____12. Making jokes about certain aspects of my life.
_____13. Making sarcastic comments about me.
_____14. Insulting me in front of other people.
_____15. Answering me with quick retorts when we're arguing.

_____16. Admonishing me harshly.

_____17. Using careless words before he thinks through how they will affect me.

_____18. Nagging me harshly.

_____19. Correcting me before he gives me a chance to fully explain a situation.

_____20. Raising his voice at me.

_____21. Making critical, illogical comments.

_____22. Swearing at me or using foul language around me.

_____23. Correcting me in public.

_____24. Being tactless when he points out my weaknesses or "blind spots."

_____25. Reminding me angrily he warned me not to do something.

_____26. Having disgusted or judgmental attitudes toward me.

_____27. Pressuring me when I'm already feeling low or offended.

_____28. Lecturing me when I need to be comforted, encouraged, or treated gently.

_____29. Breaking promises without any explanation or without asking to be released from the promise.

_____30. Telling me how wonderful other women are and comparing me to other women.

_____31. Holding onto resentment about something I did and which I tried to make right.

_____32. Being disrespectful to my family members and other relatives.

_____33. Coercing me into arguments.

_____34. Correcting or angrily punishing me for something that I'm not guilty of.

_____35. Not praising me for something that I did well, even if I did it for him.

_____36. Treating me like a child.

_____37. Being rude to me or other people when we're in public (such as restaurant personnel or store clerks.)

_____38. Being unaware of my needs.

_____39. Being ungrateful.

_____40. Not trusting me.

_____41. Not approving of what I do or of how I do it.

_____42. Not being interested in my personal growth or my spiritual growth.

_____43. Being inconsistent or having double standards (doing things he doesn't want me to do.)

_____44. Not giving me advice when I really need and ask for it.

_____45. Not telling me in specific ways that he loves me.

_____46. Having proud and arrogant attitudes in general.

_____47. Not giving me the daily encouragement that I need.

_____48. Failing to include me in conversations when we are out together with other people.

_____49. Failing to spend focused time with me when we attend social gatherings.

_____50. Continuing a discussion or arguing a point, simply

_____ to prove that he was right.

_____51. Ignoring me in our home, as if I weren't a member of the family.

_____52. Not taking time at the end of the day to listen to what is important to me.

_____53. Not paying any attention to me at social gatherings.

_____54. Not attending church with us as a family.

_____55. Failing to honestly express to me his innermost feelings.

_____56. Showing more excitement for work and other activities than for me.

_____57. Being impolite at mealtimes.

_____58. Having sloppy manners around the house or in front of others.

_____59. Not inviting me out regularly on special romantic dates. (Just the two of us.)

_____60. Not helping me with the children at extra stressful times, such as before mealtimes or at bedtime.

_____61. Not volunteering to help me with the dishes occasionally—or with cleaning the house.

_____62. Making me feel stupid when I share an idea about his work or about decisions that need to be made.

_____63. Making me feel unworthy for wanting certain furniture or insurance or other material needs for myself and for the family.

_____64. Not being consistent with the discipline of the kids.

_____65. Not taking an interest in playing with the children and not spending quality and quantity time with them.

_____66. Not showing affection for me in public, like holding my hand or putting his arm around me (like he's embarrassed to be with me.)

_____67. Not sharing his life, his ideas or his feelings with me (such as what's going on at work.)

_____68. Not being the spiritual leader of our home.

_____69. Demanding me to submit to him.

_____70. Demanding me to respond to him sexually when we're not in harmony with one another.

_____71. Being unwilling to readily admit when he's wrong.

_____72. Being defensive whenever I point out one of his "blind spots."

_____73. Being too busy with work or other activities.

_____74. Not showing compassion and understanding for the children and me when there's a real need to.

_____75. Not planning for the future, which makes me very insecure.

_____76. Being stingy with money, making me feel I have to beg for every penny.

_____77. Wanting to do things sexually, that make me feel embarrassed.

_____78. Reading pornographic magazines or watching indiscreet videos.

_____79. Forcing me to make many of the decisions

	regarding the checkbook and bills.
___80.	Forcing me to handle bill collectors and overdue bills.
___81.	Not letting me lean on his gentleness and strength (or not having gentleness and strength for me to lean on.)
___82.	Not allowing me to fail—always believing he has to correct me.
___83.	Refusing to recognize my uniqueness and my differences as a woman.
___84.	Criticizing my womanly characteristics or sensitivity as "weakness."
___85.	Spending too much money and placing the family under financial pressure.
___86.	Not having a sense of humor and not joking about things with me.
___87.	Not sending me special love letters or hand-written notes from time to time.
___88.	Forgetting special occasions such as anniversaries or birthdays.
___89.	Not defending me when someone else criticizes me or tears me down, especially if it's one of his relatives or friends.
___90.	Not putting his arms around me and hugging me when I need to be comforted.
___91.	Not bragging to other people about me.
___92.	Being dishonest.
___93.	Discouraging me when I try to better myself, either through education or through exercise.
___94.	Continuing to practice distasteful or harmful habits.
___95.	Not treating me gently.
___96.	Ignoring my relatives and the people who are important to me.
___97.	Taking me for granted; assuming that "a woman's work is never done."
___98.	Not including me in future plans until the last minute.
___99.	Seldom doing little unexpected things for me to let me know he loves me and appreciates me.
___100.	Not treating me as an intellectual equal.
___101.	Viewing me as a weaker individual in general.
___102.	Being preoccupied with his own goals and needs, and making me feel the children and I are not his top priority.
___103.	Threatening to never let me do something again because I made some mistake in the past.
___104.	Criticizing me behind my back. (This is especially painful for me if I hear about his criticism from someone else.)
___105.	Blaming me for things in our relationship that are clearly his fault.
___106.	Not being aware of my physical limitations;

treating me like a man, by roughhousing with me or making me carry heavy objects.

___107. Being impatient or angry with me when I can't keep up with his schedule or physical stamina.

___108. Acting like he's a martyr if he goes along with my opinions.

___109. Sulking when I challenge his comments.

___110. Joining too many organizations that exclude the children and me.

___111. Failing to repair items around the house.

___112. Watching too much TV and neglecting family time.

___113. Demanding me to sit down and listen to his point of view when I need to be doing other things.

___114. Insisting upon lecturing me in order to convey the importance of the points he wants to make.

___115. Humiliating me with words and actions; saying things lilke, "I can't stand to live in a messy house."

___116. Not taking the time to prepare me to enjoy sexual intimacy.

___117. Spending money extravagantly, without faithfully giving to God.

___118. Avoiding family activities that the children enjoy.

___119. Taking vacations that are primarily what he wants to do.

___120. Not letting me get away to spend time with friends, go shopping, go out for coffee and dessert at a restaurant, etc.

___121. Refusing to join me in the things I enjoy, like shopping, going out for coffee and dessert, etc.

___122. Not understanding the challenging responsibilities a wife has: laundry, cooking, picking up clothes and toys all day long, wiping runny noses, changing diapers, etc.

___123. Refusing to be self-sacrificial by regularly touching me in non-sexual ways, solely for my pleasure and enjoyment, not leading to sexual intercourse.

"A Husband's Checklist of Offenses"

Many husbands need to forgive their wives before God, for the offenses their wives have committed against them.

This chapter examines the widespread resentment many men feel because they haven't forgiven their wives for offending them. It's necessary for a husband to specifically identify the areas in which his wife has hurt him, so he can thoroughly forgive her.

The following is a list of 110 ways that wives typically hurt their husbands. Review the list carefully and select the statements that apply to your individual situation. Then forgive your wife before God so bitterness won't defile your life.

I forgive my wife for:

____1. Expecting me to know what she needs without telling me.
____2. Ignoring me.
____3. Trying to be financially independent.
____4. Not valuing my opinions.
____5. Insisting on maintaining separate checking accounts.
____6. Paying more attention to other people than to me.
____7. Demonstrating greater loyalty to others (parents, children, employer, friends, pastor, etc.) than to me.
____8. Resisting my decisions in her heart.
____9. Resisting my physical affection.
____10. Making me feel guilty if I desire her sexually when she doesn't desire me.
____11. Being unresponsive to me sexually.
____12. Withholding sex as a means of punishing me for my insensitivity or wrong behavior.
____13. Taking my responsibilities into her hands in order to see to it that they get done.
____14. Not respecting me as a person in a God-given position of authority over her.
____15. Not respecting me as the God-given leader in our home.
____16. Not expressing confidence in me when I make wrong decisions.
____17. Not showing loyalty and support in spite of the wrong decisions I make.
____18. Not appreciating me for the positive things that I do for her or for the family.
____19. Not expressing enthusiasm for my achievements.
____20. Being inattentive to me when I'm talking.

_____21. Not taking care of her physical appearance and/or health.
_____22. Not being determined to develop a gentle and contented spirit, which God says is precious.
_____23. Failing to know or apply the biblical principles of appeal when she needs to appeal to me about certain situations.
_____24. Being unwilling to forgive me for past failures or hurts.
_____25. Being unwilling to explain her needs and fears without condemning me.
_____26. Being unwilling to define her responsibilities to me.
_____27. Discrediting or criticizing me to other people.
_____28. Failing to encourage me to spend time alone with the Lord.
_____29. Condemning me for not being the spiritual leader of our family and for not taking more spiritual responsibility.
_____30. Not understanding that a man's need to spend time alone with God is rejecting her.
_____31. Being unwilling to learn contentment in her present circumstances.
_____32. Being ungrateful for each expression of my love or provision.
_____33. Not praising me for growth or achievement in areas where she wants me to improve.
_____34. Not visualizing how our marriage problems are helping her achieve greater character and growth in her relationship with Jesus Christ.
_____35. Making sarcastic comments about me.
_____36. Insulting me in front of others.
_____37. Using careless words when she communicates with me.
_____38. Nagging me harshly.
_____39. Raising her voice at me.
_____40. Making critical comments that seem to have no basis.
_____41. Swearing at me or using foul language in my presence.
_____42. Correcting me in public.
_____43. Being tactless when she points out my weaknesses or blind spots.
_____44. Reminding me angrily that she warned me not to do something.
_____45. Having disgusted or judgmental attitudes.
_____46. Telling me how wonderful other men are and comparing me to them.
_____47. Being disrespectful to my family members and other relatives.
_____48. Coercing me into arguments.
_____49. Not praising me for something I did well, even if I did it for her.
_____50. Treating me like a child.
_____51. Being unaware of my needs.

____52. Not trusting me.

____53. Not approving of what I do or how I do it in a general sense.

____54. Not being interested in her own personal growth or spiritual growth.

____55. Not giving me input when I really need and ask for it.

____56. Not telling me that she loves me in specific ways.

____57. Having generally selfish and condemning attitudes.

____58. Not attending church regularly.

____59. Showing more excitement for work and other activities than for me.

____60. Not being consistent with the discipline of the kids.

____61. Being unwilling to admit when she is wrong.

____62. Being defensive when I point out one of her "blind spots."

____63. Being too busy with work and other activities.

____64. Not allowing me to fail—believing that she always has to correct me.

____65. Spending too much money and accumulating too much debt.

____66. Not having a sense of humor and not being able to joke about things.

____67. Not telling me how important I am to her.

____68. Not defending me when someone else complains about me or tears me down, (especially if it is one of her relatives or friends.)

____69. Not praising me to other people.

____70. Ignoring my relatives and the people who are important to me.

____71. Criticizing me behind my back. (This is especially painful for me if I hear about her criticism from someone else.)

____72. Blaming me for the things in our relationship that are clearly her fault.

____73. Becoming impatient or angry with me when I can't keep up with her schedule or her physical stamina.

____74. Acting like she's a martyr if she goes along with my decisions.

____75. Sulking when I challenge her comments.

____76. Insisting upon lecturing me in order to convey the importance of her points.

____77. Putting other things before me.

____78. Showing more appreciation or admiration for other men than for me.

____79. Criticizing or belittling my character or abilities.

____80. Pushing me to do things that I think shouldn't be done.

____81. Making fun of my leadership (even in jest.)

____82. Not seeking my advice or counsel on issues in her world.

____83. Allowing trivial and non-essential discussions to become arguments.

____84. Constantly complaining.

_____85. Honoring her parents above me.
_____86. Devaluing my input with the children.
_____87. Complaining about the time that I need with other men to pursue positive goals.
_____88. Being uninterested in my recreational interests.
_____89. Violating money management agreements.
_____90. Not generally admiring me as a man.
_____91. Not respecting my leadership.
_____92. Berating me for lack of spiritual leadership.
_____93. Not paying full attention while I am talking to her.
_____94. Interrupting me before she has heard me out.
_____95. Trying to get in the last word in order to win an argument.
_____96. Using statements like "You always," and "You never."
_____97. Devaluing my vocation or work pursuits.
_____98. Failing to take care of her physical appearance.
_____99. Failing to assume her part of the responsibility to keep the house neat and clean.
_____100. Making fun of my physical appearance.
_____101. Not building me up and not encouraging me.
_____102. Not expressing a gentle and respectful spirit when we disagree.
_____103. Bringing up past failures and hurts.
_____104. Arguing with me or questioning me in front of the kids.
_____105. Consistently putting the children's needs before mine.
_____106. Keeping secrets from me and being untrustworthy.
_____107. Making excuses about the children's disobedience.
_____108. Excessive spending and use of credit cards.
_____109. Forgetting things that matter to me.
_____110. Not praying for me.

"A Child's Checklist of Offenses"

In order to forgive his parents fully, a child must acknowledge the offenses they have committed against him.

God instructs parents not to provoke their children to anger. Many children feel resentment toward their parents, but they deny that they've allowed a root of bitterness to grow in their hearts. Once a child lists the specific ways his parents have hurt him, he can then specifically and thoroughly forgive his parents before God.

Listed below are 86 offenses that parents typically commit against their children. As children read through this list, they should check the items that apply to their individual situation. Then they should use those items as a guide to specifically forgive their parents.

I forgive my parents for:

____1. Imposing discipline that they later wished they had not imposed.
____2. "Calling me names" in an attempt to correct me.
____3. Not always encouraging me to be all that I can be.
____4. Often being inattentive to me when I am speaking to them.
____5. Sometimes implying that I am stupid for not already having certain knowledge or information when they are instructing me.
____6. Not attempting to understand the reasons why I get angry.
____7. Failing to instruct me when I have been disobedient.
____8. Not allowing me to make an increasing number of decisions on my own.
____9. Nagging me to coerce me to do things.
____10. Not allowing me to feel the consequences of my mistakes.
____11. Belittling me to other people (brothers, sisters, family members, friends, etc.)
____12. Not allowing me to enter into adult conversations.
____13. Failing to accept and respect the differences in temperaments and personality traits between my siblings and me.
____14. Punishing me in anger.
____15. Disciplining me inconsistently.
____16. Seldom asking me for forgiveness.
____17. Not encouraging me when I am disappointed or

discouraged.

____18. Speaking negatively about my friends.

____19. Using sarcasm as a means of discipline.

____20. Not requiring me to make restitution when it is appropriate for me to do so.

____21. Spanking me in front of other people (siblings, friends, other family members, etc.)

____22. Not helping me appreciate my unique abilities.

____23. Not showing me the same courtesy they show others.

____24. Threatening to carry out certain acts of discipline, but failing to follow through.

____25. Frequently overreacting to me or to situations.

____26. Sometimes being out of control when they spank me.

____27. Losing their tempers in front of me.

____28. Not encouraging and supporting my personal interests.

____29. Resorting to yelling and screaming as part of their method for controlling or disciplining me.

____30. Withdrawing their affection from me after disciplining me.

____31. Not praising me when I choose not to repeat a bad behavior after I had the opportunity to do so.

____32. Failing to pay me frequent compliments.

____33. Holding a grudge against me.

____34. Saying with the tone of their voice, "Go away. I don't want to be bothered."

____35. Not making clear who the leader is in our home.

____36. Using a lot of emotionalism to solve problems in our home.

____37. Not usually hearing or accepting my ideas and suggestions for problem solving.

____38. Not usually allowing me to "have my own opinion."

____39. Sometimes playing favorites with my siblings and me.

____40. Sometimes not giving me the attention that I need.

____41. Sometimes making me feel less important than other people in our home.

____42. Sometimes using intimidation as a disciplinary measure.

____43. Not giving me the opportunity to learn to pray by listening to their prayers.

____44. Being inconsistent in reading Christian literature aloud to me.

____45. Being inconsistent in their personal devotional time.

____46. Seldom using the Bible to make decisions in our family.

____47. Seldom praying together as a family, except at mealtimes.

____48. Not having regular family devotions.

____49. Not regularly witnessing to lost people.

____50. Not memorizing Scripture together as a family.

____51. Not consistently teaching me the biblical principles for living an obedient Christian life.

____52. Not having a good understanding of how my needs change, as I get older.

____53. Not knowing my friends' names.

____54. Rarely having time to play games with me.

____55. Not spending time individually with me, doing things that I enjoy.

___ 56. Not looking me in the eye when I talk to them.

___57. Not expressing appropriate physical affection for me by hugging and touching me.

___58. Not telling me that I am special to them.

___59. Not pointing out positive character qualities that they see in me.

___60. Often varying their approach in how they deal with me.

___61. Seldom telling me what to expect from them.

___62. Seldom sacrificing personal time to be with me.

___63. Not being as involved as they should be with my discipline.

___64. Not making an effort to keep the romance alive in their marriage.

___65. Not making an effort to maintain a good relationship with one another.

___66. Hitting me in anger.

___67. Not taking an active role in my education.

___68. Not touching or hugging me every day.

___69. Not telling me on a consistent basis that they are proud of me.

___70. Not being a good role model for me.

___71. Not consistently modeling the kind of behavior that I should imitate.

___72. Not responding calmly when I say hurtful things or when I act disobediently.

___73. Not teaching me how to respond if I disagree with them.

___74. Not making an effort to improve their parenting skills, by attending classes, reading books, etc.

___75. Bribing me with a reward for good behavior, such as, "If you behave we'll go to McDonalds."

Check any number below that applies to you:

___76. I feel like my relationship with my parents is hopeless.

___77. I don't settle disagreements with my parents quickly enough.

___78. I'm afraid to "get involved" in a close relationship with my parents.

___79. I'm afraid to let my parents know who I really am.

___80. My past mistakes have damaged my relationship with my parents.

___81. I feel like I'm my parents' slave.

___82. I'm afraid my parents will abandon me.

___83. I don't feel my parents accept or understand me.

___84. I sense a "distance" in my relationship with my parents.

___85. I don't communicate with my parents.

___86. I don't feel like my parents are "on my side."

"A Parent's Checklist of Offenses"

In order to forgive their children fully, parents must identify the specific ways their children have offended them.

Is your home a war zone? Parents are often offended by their children's disobedience and disrespectful attitudes. Many teenagers are disenchanted with their family life. They don't like the rules their parents impose on them, they don't care for their parents' discipline, and they believe they're the victims of inhumane, unfair treatment.

Use this checklist to help identify the specific ways your children have offended you. Then prayerfully use these questions as a tool to help you forgive your children.

I forgive my children for:

_____ 1. Telling me "no" when I give them a command.

_____ 2. Interrupting my conversations when my spouse and I are talking to each other or other adults.

_____ 3. Complaining when I give them a job to do.

_____ 4. Waiting to obey, or procrastinating (putting off obeying until later).

_____ 5. Arguing with me.

_____ 6. Demonstrating an ungrateful spirit to me by complaining about food, clothes, shoes, etc.

_____ 7. Comparing me to their friends' parents.

_____ 8. Talking back to me.

_____ 9. Rolling their eyes in disgust at me, or making other unacceptable facial expressions.

_____ 10. Showing disrespect for me by talking about me negatively to others.

_____ 11. Doing the jobs I give them half-heartedly, just to "get by".

_____ 12 Trying to manipulate me to get their way.

_____ 13. Lying to me.

_____ 14. Telling me "half-truths" (which is still deception).

_____ 15. Not calling me to let me know when they'll be late coming home.

_____ 16. Doing things that I don't approve of.

_____ 17. Stealing things.

_____ 18. Trading their possessions with friends, without my permission.

_____ 19. Seeing movies, or videos that they know I would not approve of.

_____ 20. Borrowing things without my approval.

_____ 21. Yelling at me or speaking rudely and disrespectfully to me.

_____ 22. Using unreasonable terms such as, "You *always*..." or "You *never*..."

_____ 23. Misusing furniture, such as slamming doors, hitting walls, throwing things, etc.

_____ 24. Pouting when they don't get their way.

_____ 25. Giving in to moods, and acting sulky.

_____ 26. Neglecting their duties, and making excuses for laziness.

_____ 27. Failing to show appreciation to me.

_____ 28. Refusing to willingly and cheerfully receive instruction or correction. (unteachable)

_____ 29. Getting out of bed at night for unnecessary reasons in order to delay going to sleep at their appointed bedtime.

_____ 30. Making long-distance phone calls without permission.

_____ 31. Abusing phone privileges; having long conversations; monopolizing family phone.

_____ 32. Spending excessive amounts of time at the computer, emailing friends, etc.

_____ 33. Doing anything illegal either in our home or outside of it.

_____ 34. Having guests over at inappropriate times.

_____ 35. Not taking proper care of their possessions and their room.

_____ 36. Misquoting what I say, to their brothers and sisters.

_____ 37. Not serving with a good attitude.

_____ 38. Always having to be reminded of their responsibilities.

_____ 39. Nagging me, or begging for something after I have said, "No."

_____ 40. Leaving certain areas of the house messy, for other people to clean up.

_____ 41. Playing tricks on me.

_____ 42. Accusing me of "playing favorites."

_____ 43. Seldom or never hugging me and telling me that they love me.

_____ 44. Seldom or never allowing me to hug them.

_____ 45. Ignoring me when I am speaking to them.

_____ 46. Responding slowly when I call them.

_____ 47. Trying to play my spouse and me against each other.

_____ 48. Not helping take care of me when I am not feeling well.

_____ 49. Trying to talk their way out of punishment that they know they deserve.

_____ 50. Having a demanding attitude, insisting upon having their way.

_____ 51. Not giving me the courtesy of their full attention when I am talking to them.

_____ 52. Wasting time in front of the TV and/or playing computer games.

_____ 53. Seldom or never asking me if there is anything special that that they can do for me.

_____ 54. Not surprising me with gifts or cards on special occasions, such as my birthday, anniversary, Mother's Day or Father's Day.

_____ 55. Not verbally expressing their appreciation to me for all that I do for them.

_____ 56. Not asking for my forgiveness when they offend me.

_____ 57. Not readily forgiving me when I offend them.

_____ 58. Not allowing me to be human and make mistakes.

_____ 59. Holding grudges against me.

_____ 60. Not praying for me.

_____ 61. Not doing their best to make good grades at school.

_____ 62. Dressing wildly, in a way that embarrasses me.

_____ 63. Being unwilling to change their hairstyle if I tell them I think it looks rebellious.

_____ 64. Not asking for my opinions about issues in their lives.

_____ 65. Refusing to get an after-school job to earn spending money.

_____ 66. Treating my friends impolitely and disrespectfully.

_____ 67. Having poor phone manners.

_____ 68. Not joining in enthusiastically on family outings.

_____ 69. Acting embarrassed to be seen with me.

_____ 70. Being insensitive to my feelings.

_____ 71. Not taking care of my possessions when they borrow them.

_____ 72. Not offering me extra help when they know I am under unusual stress.

_____ 73. Never offering to run errands for me.

_____ 74. Borrowing money from me and "forgetting" to pay it back.

_____ 75. Seldom or never paying me compliments.

_____ 76. Losing things and expecting me to replace them.

_____ 77. Automatically blaming me when something goes wrong.

_____ 78. Pitching temper tantrums.

_____ 79. Exaggerating stories or "stretching the truth" when I ask them questions about their life.

_____ 80. Muttering things under their breath when I rebuke them.

Resources

To order these books, visit us on the Web at:
biblicalcounseling.com

You Are Your Sister's Keeper (Uncomplicated Ministering, Girlfriend to Girlfriend) [$12]
by Dr. Debbi Dunlap

Description: Mentoring! God calls women to invest their lives in faith-cultivating relationships with other women. Yet who has time or motivation to commit to another training program? So Debbi has done the footwork to save you prep time as you minister to the complex needs women face today. Not a front-to-back read, this "cafeteria-style" book contains principles and related scriptures addressing aspects of every woman's faith journey. Whatever topic you're dealing with, you'll find a concise, substantive "jumping-off" guide in this exciting new resource. Written by an experienced pastor's wife/mother of 10, this book is a gold-mine for women dedicated to initiating meaningful faith-cultivating relationships.

Straighten Up and Fly Right Parents! (Getting Spiritual Backbone to Discipline Your Kids) [$9]
By Drs. Don and Debbi Dunlap

Description: "You have to the count of three to obey me!" Do those words sound familiar? How about, "Do as I say, not as I do!" Or that time-honored threat, "You're grounded!" Interested in finding out why all these disciplinary techniques are ineffective? The authors have ten children and more parenting experience than they bargained for! If you're held hostage by disrespectful, unruly kids, this little power-packed book could rescue you! Don, an experienced and trusted family counselor, and Debbi, a women's conference leader, will help you understand the biblical principles of child discipline.

Help! I Married FrankenSpouse (Fixing Your Marriage Before It Becomes a Horror Story) [$9]
By Drs. Don and Debbi Dunlap

Description: After a few years (or less!) of marriage, lots of husbands and wives feel they're not married to the same person they exchanged wedding vows with. The authors, respected and experienced family counselors, help you unravel this mystery and make your way back to a fulfilling marriage relationship. Spouse "Offense" checklists, and several chapters on dealing with the devastating effects of adultery make this little book an absolute must-buy!

Stop Acting Like a Baby! (Dealing with Anger—God's Way) [$9]
By Drs. Don and Debbi Dunlap

Description: Seems no matter where we go these days, we usually end up witnessing an angry shouting match, or hearing foul, uncensored language anytime someone is the least bit provoked. It's suddenly OK for adults to pitch angry fits (like grown-up babies) to get their anger out, if that's what works for them. But the truth hasn't changed: unbridled anger is deadly when it comes to maintaining solid, meaningful, nurturing relationships. This book offers you an effective, biblical plan to deal with anger in a way that enhances relationships, and enlarges the scope of your Christian testimony.

About the Author

Don Dunlap, former Senior Editor for Counseling and feature writer on counseling and family for the Christianity.com Network, has conducted over 25,000 counseling appointments during his ministerial career. A leading Pastoral Counselor and pioneer in the placement of Pastoral Counselors in the offices of Christian physicians, Don is founder and director of Family Physician Partners, and has established offices in South Carolina, North Carolina, Alabama, Georgia, and Florida.

As the Director of Family Counseling Ministries, with headquarters in Jacksonville, Florida, Don conducts Family Life Conferences, Parent Training Seminars, and Marriage Enrichment Retreats.

Don has a degree in Child Development from Florida State University, and a Master's Degree in Education and Theology (specializing in Marriage and Family Counseling) from Southwestern Baptist Theological Seminary. He holds a Doctor of Ministry degree from Luther Rice Seminary. His counseling practice includes adults, children, and families in crisis. Don also provides telephone counseling for individuals who are unable to meet face-to-face with a competent, Bible-based counselor.

Don has authored several books, and written numerous articles related to marriage and family. You can contact him at his website, www.biblicalcounseling.com

Author's Testimony

I became a Christian in high school through the outreach ministry of Campus Crusade for Christ. They immediately challenged me to begin sharing my faith with others, and to get involved in discipleship training and ministry equipping. Within a few months of my 16th birthday, I decided to prepare for pastoral ministry.

After completing my undergraduate degree I attended Seminary with the goal of acquiring the knowledge, resources, and skills to effectively minister God's Word in pastoral work. I got married during my final year of Seminary.

Like many young men, I came to marriage thoroughly unprepared for the responsibilities I had assumed. Although Debbi and I were both committed Christians, neither of us had a very clear understanding of how to apply the Scriptures to our daily lives. Soon after marriage we began to experience serious conflict. Unresolved bitterness and resentment began to surface dramatically in both our lives.

Over the next several years, we experienced the consequences of not having received a strong biblical foundation early on in our walk with Christ. Our problems continued to intensify and eventually we found ourselves considering divorce. Through God's mercy and the loving intervention of godly counselors, our marriage was salvaged.

I often tell counselees that I wish I could sit before them with a testimony of a successful life, marriage, and ministry. But that's not the case. The truth of the matter is, I sit before them with a message of failure and weakness. Praise His name that He makes Himself strong in our weakness. Where there was brokenness and humiliation, He provided forgiveness and restoration. My greatest hope lies in this extraordinary promise: "God comforts us in our troubles so that we can comfort others with the comfort we have received."

I know the pain and heartbreak of a difficult marriage. And I know the miracle of God granting beauty for ashes. The Lord has given Debbi and me success in our marriage relationship as we've cried out to Him for help, sought godly mentors, and made our lives accountable to fellow Believers.

For the past several years I've met weekly with a group of Christian men. I've submitted my life, my marriage, and my ministry to their scrutiny and prayerful support, and I thank God for their consistent, continual love and encouragement.

I am very grateful for the ministry of Dr. Howard Hendricks. He has significantly impacted my life. His life and teaching have given me a blueprint for how to be the spiritual head of my home, how to love and cherish my wife, and how to raise my children.

I remain in the debt of Dr. Jay Adams. His books have provided the theological basis for my ongoing counseling ministry. His life and mentoring provided the example of a loving, nurturing pastor, for which my family and I are profoundly grateful.